Let's Draw!

★ A fun guide to drawing everything! ★

ARCTURUS

ARCTURUS

This edition published in 2014 by Arcturus Publishing Limited
26/27 Bickels Yard, 151–153 Bermondsey Street,
London SE1 3HA

Illustrated by Peter Gray
Designed by Picnic Design
Written by Deborah Kespert
Edited by Anna Brett

ISBN: 978-1-84837-839-1
CH001760UK
Supplier 05, Date 0114, Print Run 3007

Printed in Singapore

CONTENTS

INTRODUCTION

Ready, steady, go!

Always wanted to know how to draw? This book is the perfect starting point as it's packed full of ideas, inspiration and simple step-by-step guides. Whether you want to improve your skills or pick up some tips, just dive in!

CHAPTERS INCLUDE

ANIMALS

From a cool chameleon to a roaring tiger and a sleek racehorse, there's an animal here for everyone.

PEOPLE

Drawing people can be a challenge, but we'll show you how. Try portraits, full figures and action poses.

MONSTERS

Let your imagination run riot by drawing loads of monsters including zombies, werewolves, dragons and sea serpents.

FANTASY CHARACTERS

Here you'll have a chance to draw both heroes and villains. How about pitting a superhero against an orc or vampire?

SPEED MACHINES

If technical drawing is your thing, then give the racing cars, speedboats and space rockets in this chapter a go.

DINOSAURS

As well as terrifying T. rex, get stuck into Triceratops, Velociraptor and Iguanodon, or try a prehistoric scene.

STYLES

REALISTIC STYLE

There are two styles of art in this book. The dinosaur above has been drawn and coloured in a realistic style with pencils and watercolour paints. Paying attention to detail and looking for references to copy helps with realistic drawings.

CARTOON STYLE

This dinosaur is quite different! It has been drawn and coloured in a cartoon style. The features are exagerrated and there is a thick black outline. Cartoon drawings allow you to experiment with shapes and colours as much as you want.

FOLLOW THE LINES

Build up your picture step-by-step by looking at the colour of each stroke. Red strokes show you the lines you need to draw and black strokes show what you have already drawn. All the lines will be red in the first step. After that only the new lines will be in red.

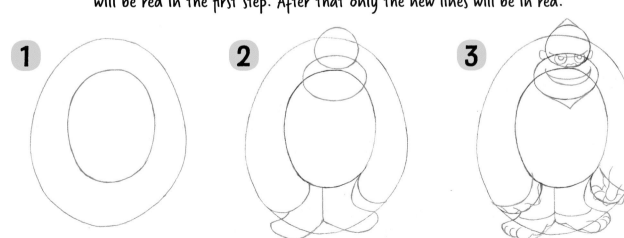

INTRODUCTION
You will need

Every artist needs essential drawing tools including pencils, pens, a ruler, paints and paper. As you become more experienced, you can add materials such as ink pens, gouache paints or pastel crayons. They will help you to develop your own favourite style.

PENCILS
Pencils come with different weights of lead. Hard lead pencils (H to 9H) are useful for drawing precise, fine lines. Soft lead pencils (B to 9B) work well for shading and softer lines.

MARKER PENS
Before colouring-in, it's a good idea to go over your pencil outline. A marker pen is perfect for this and you can use a thick or thin one depending on the effect you want to create.

PAPER
You can use different types of paper for different jobs. When practising shapes and lines, a rough sketch paper is practical. For final coloured-up drawings, a smooth plain paper works well.

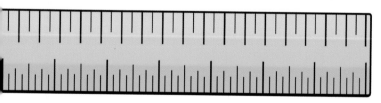

RULER
For technical drawings, a ruler really helps. It will allow you to make your lines straight and angles accurate.

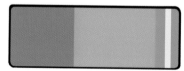

ERASER
From time to time, you'll make mistakes or need to rub out guidelines. That's where an eraser comes in handy. Don't worry if you make mistakes, everybody does!

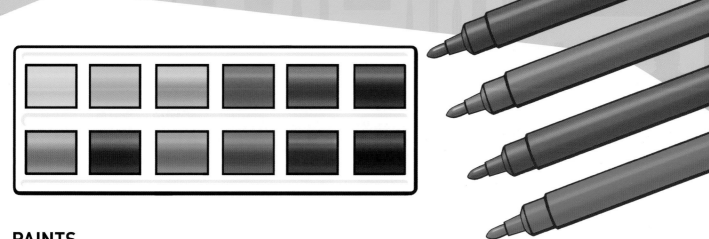

PAINTS

There are all different kinds of paints you can experiment with but poster paints and watercolours are an excellent starting point. You could also try gouache, which will give you more solid tones.

FELT-TIP PENS

Felt-tips are perfect for colouring drawings that need bold, bright colours. They work especially well for cartoons.

ART IN ACTION

Take a look at the examples below to see how to get the best out of using different pens, brushes and paints.

This friendly dolphin was coloured in watercolour paints to give a smooth effect. Colours can be blended together to create different shades with watercolours.

Felt-tip pens were used to colour this cartoon shark, making it look dramatic. The outline was done with a fine black marker pen and the body was highlighted with white chalk.

INTRODUCTION
Shapes and lines

All the drawings in this book start with simple shapes and lines. They give you a basic structure to build on. Then you can work on developing the details.

SIMPLE SHAPES

Here are some examples of the shapes you'll use. It's a good idea to practise drawing them until you feel comfortable. For some of the shapes, such as the squares, rectangles and triangles, use a ruler to get straight lines.

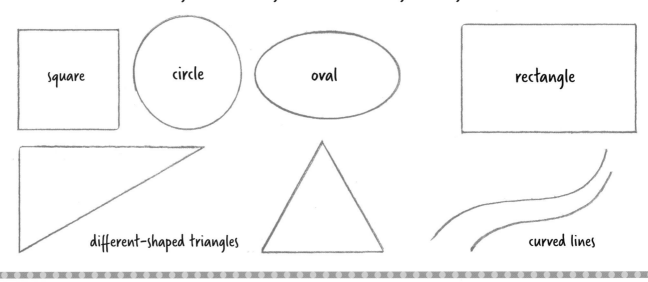

square

circle

oval

rectangle

different-shaped triangles

curved lines

BUILD IT UP
Once you've mastered drawing shapes, the next step is to build them up into a real picture. This fighter jet is made from different-shaped triangles and straight lines that have been smoothed and softened in places.

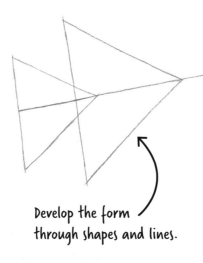

Develop the form through shapes and lines.

Then soften the edges to make the jet real. You'll need your eraser at this stage.

LINES

THICK LINES

You can create different effects depending on the thickness of your line. This tiger looks dramatic because it has a thick bold outline and fur made with jagged short strokes.

SMUDGED LINES

Smudging your lines makes this werewolf seem wild as it gives the fur a sense of movement. Try soft pencil or charcoal, then smudge the line with your finger. You could also use an old brush and ink to get a scratchy effect.

FINE LINES

A fine line gives a more delicate appearance. It's perfect for creating the whispy fur on this almost cuddly yeti. Notice how the outline is not solid but made up of lots of tiny strokes drawn very close together.

Colour magic

When you colour in your drawings, you instantly bring them to life. As well as working with colours that go well together, think about those that contrast. Using colour is also a great way to create a particular mood or feel.

If you're going for realistic hair, then it's a good idea to avoid a single block of colour. Brown, yellow and white have all been blended together here.

Did you know that you can make brown by blending green and red together. Try this with watercolour paints.

To give this elf a truly woodland feel, we decided to colour in her outfit entirely in different shades of green.

To add some 'zing' to the picture, try including a touch of lime green. You can make this by blending a strong green with bright yellow.

COLOUR WHEEL

A colour wheel can help you decide how to mix and match colour. The primary colours are red, yellow and blue and you can make up all the other colours by mixing them.

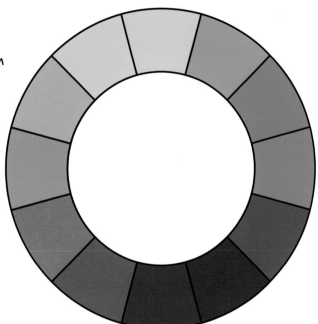

Colours that sit next to each other, such as blue and green and red and orange, go well together and create almost no contrast.

Colours that sit opposite each other, such as red and green, and purple and yellow provide lots of contrast. They are called complementary colours.

Warm colours are much richer. They include yellow, orange and red.

Cool colours can create a sense of calm. These include blue and green.

CUDDLY AND CUTE
Changing the colour of a picture or adding features can make a huge difference. This green baby dragon looks friendly and sweet.

HOT AND BOTHERED
Turn him bright red and he becomes more mischievous. Give him a puff of fire and you know not to anger him!

Shading and

Adding darker areas of colour to a picture is called shading. Highlights are patches of white. Artists use these techniques to give their pictures bulk and depth so they seem three-dimensional and real. Find out how on the Triceratops example below.

A wobbly outline helps to create a bony backbone.

1 Once you have outlined your drawing, plot out where the shading needs to go. Darker areas around the neck, underneath the body and on the legs give this dinosaur its bulk.

2 Now build up the shading. We have used a watercolour paint because we are working in a realistic style. Make sure that the shading is in a darker colour than the main body colour.

Notice how the brush strokes curve and round out the body.

Wrinkly lines give the skin texture.

highlights

3 Now cover the whole picture with the main body colour, in this case a light brown. Notice how by going over the whole body, including the shaded areas, the colours feel blended together.

A brown outline makes the bony neck plate look solid.

4 The final step is to add highlights. Here we have used white chalk on top of the watercolour. Add most of the highlights around the neck plate, spiny back and thigh joints to make them stand out.

Curve your highlights and follow the body shape.

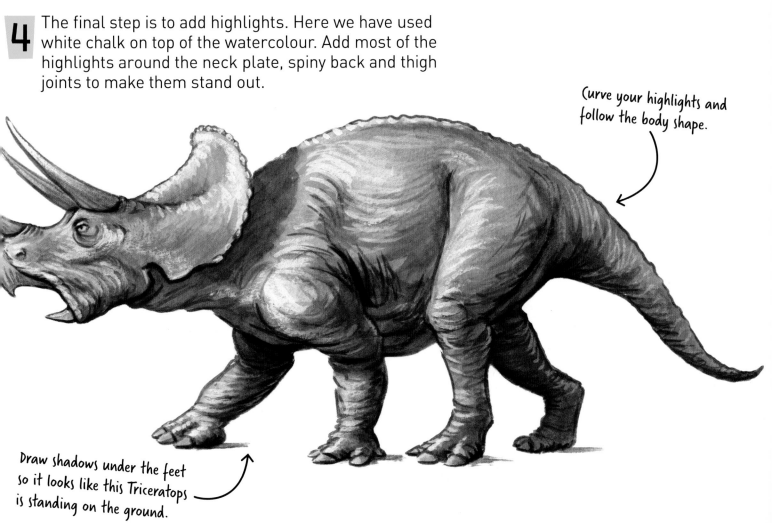

Draw shadows under the feet so it looks like this Triceratops is standing on the ground.

INTRODUCTION
Perspective

In real life, objects look smaller the further away they are. You can create this feel in your pictures by drawing them in perspective. Using this technique will also help make the objects look solid. Follow the steps below to find out how.

VANISHING POINTS

When creating perspective, you need at least one vanishing point. This is the point where parallel lines would meet in the distance if you kept on looking at them.

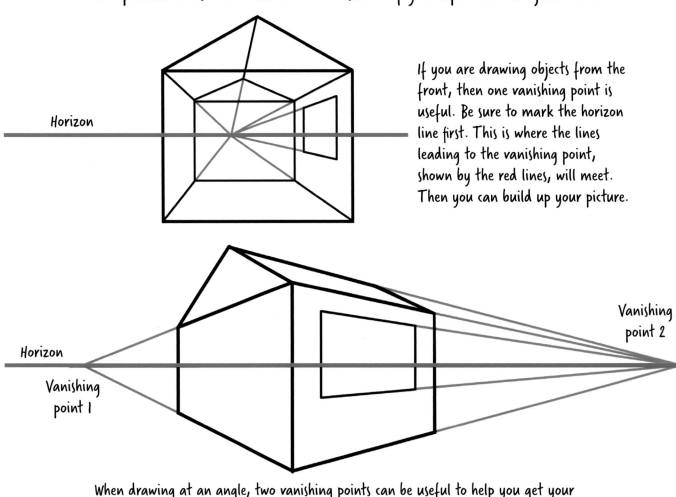

If you are drawing objects from the front, then one vanishing point is useful. Be sure to mark the horizon line first. This is where the lines leading to the vanishing point, shown by the red lines, will meet. Then you can build up your picture.

When drawing at an angle, two vanishing points can be useful to help you get your picture right. Both of the vanishing points should be positioned on the horizon line.

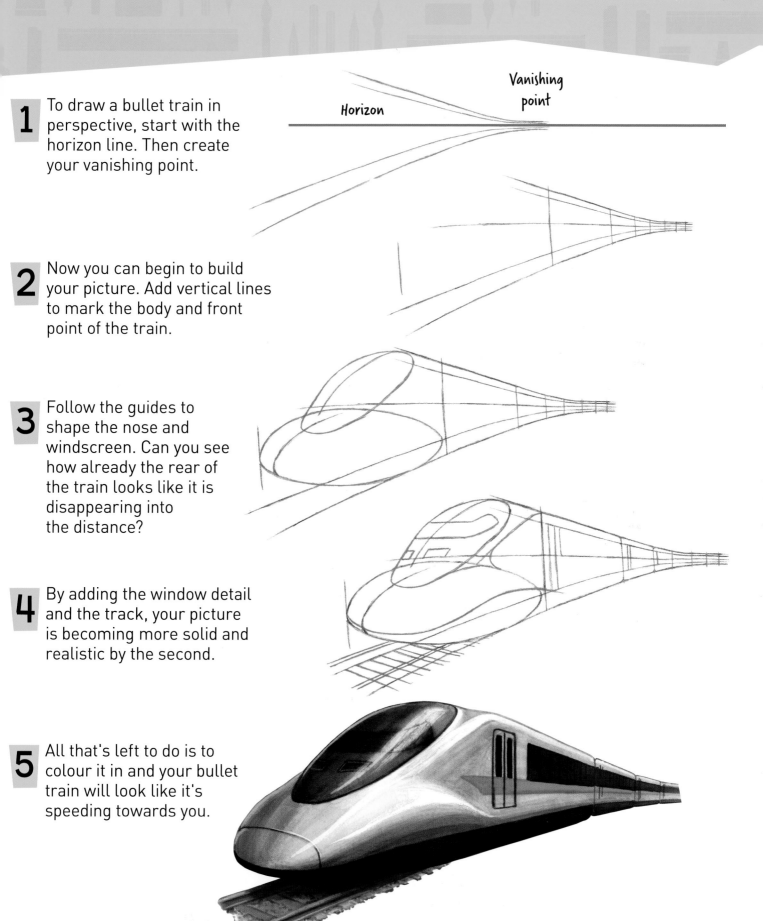

1. To draw a bullet train in perspective, start with the horizon line. Then create your vanishing point.

Horizon

Vanishing point

2. Now you can begin to build your picture. Add vertical lines to mark the body and front point of the train.

3. Follow the guides to shape the nose and windscreen. Can you see how already the rear of the train looks like it is disappearing into the distance?

4. By adding the window detail and the track, your picture is becoming more solid and realistic by the second.

5. All that's left to do is to colour it in and your bullet train will look like it's speeding towards you.

INTRODUCTION
The next step

At the end of each chapter, you have the chance to create a whole scene based on some of the material you have drawn before. We'll include hints and tips so you can use these pages as a springboard for creating more fantastic scenes of your own.

BUILD A LAB

On pages 82–3, you draw a nutty professor, then on page 92, you put him in his whacky lab. Try adding backgrounds for your other fantasy characters. The elf princess could live in a woodland glade and the vampire a spooky castle!

DESIGN A RACETRACK

You find out how to draw the red sports car on pages 94–5, then on page 110, we show you how to put it on a race track. How about using your other speed machines to create a jet plane display or a motorbike stunt course?

ANIMALS

The animal kingdom is full of different kinds of incredible creatures. From mammals and birds to reptiles, insects and fish, you'll have the chance to draw them all!

Racehorse

Find out how to create shiny sleek fur when you tackle this powerful racehorse on the move.

Crocodile

Have some fun with this scaly cartoon croc and give him different expressions.

Dolphin

Work on developing a smooth streamlined body to bring this friendly dolphin to life.

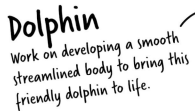

Owl

As well as this swooping owl, there's also a colourful rainforest toucan to draw.

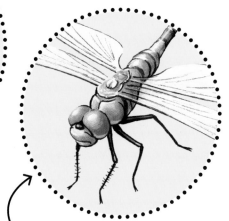

Dragonfly

Draw and colour a darting dragonfly, then create a whole pond scene for it to fly over.

Galloping horse

A sleek racehorse uses its powerful muscles to gallop along. This horse has a shiny, dark brown coat but your horse's coat could be light brown, black, white or dappled grey.

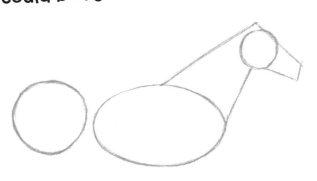

1 Start with a circle and an oval for the body. Draw two lines to form a thick neck, paying attention to their angles. Add a smaller circle and rectangle for the head.

2 Create galloping legs and a tail with curved lines. Add small circles for the leg joints, spacing them out carefully. Draw semicircles for the hooves.

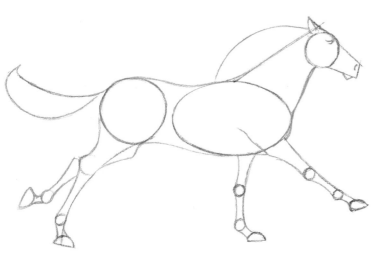

3 Use curved lines to create an outline. Draw the final back leg, and shape the head, mane and tail. Don't forget to include the features on the face too.

4 Carefully rub out the basic shapes and finish off the detail. By adding more flowing lines to the mane and tail you can create a sense of movement.

5 Colour the horse a rich brown and blend it into black. Use hints of white to show off its muscles.

TOP TIPS

Add a professional touch to your racehorse by following these extra tips.

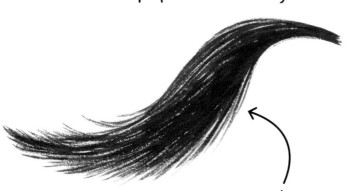

For the perfect swishing tail, press firmly and smoothly with your pencil to make lots of curved lines. Then shade the centre.

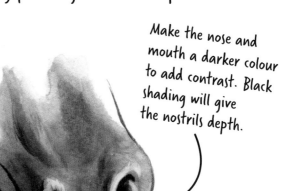

Make the nose and mouth a darker colour to add contrast. Black shading will give the nostrils depth.

Tiger face

Get up-close and personal with a roaring tiger! Do your best to capture the fierce expression on this cartoon face by spending time on the eyes, nose and teeth.

1 Draw a wide oval for the head. Then add lines down and across the middle to help you position the features. Carefully copy the shapes for the eyes, nose and mouth, making sure they are in the right places.

2 Next start to develop the face. Give the mouth four long, sharp teeth and a tongue Work on the eyes and the nose. Then add the ears and outline the top of the head.

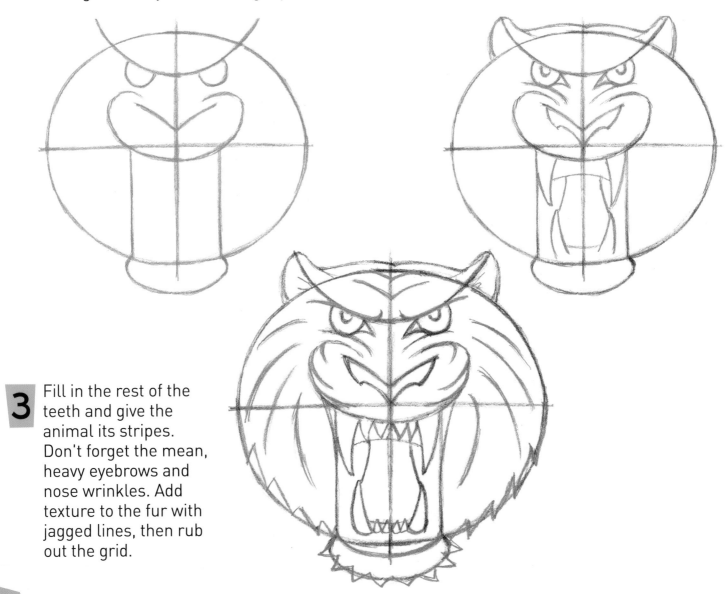

3 Fill in the rest of the teeth and give the animal its stripes. Don't forget the mean, heavy eyebrows and nose wrinkles. Add texture to the fur with jagged lines, then rub out the grid.

4 Go over the fur with a black felt-tip pen, using jagged strokes for the stripes. Make the eyes and mouth really dark. Then colour in the tiger.

CARTOON CORNER

Transform your roaring tiger into a gentle giant or even another big cat!

1 For a gentle tiger, lose the nose wrinkles and make the eyebrows shorter. Draw a curved, closed mouth.

2 If you add a shaggy mane to your gentle tiger and lose the stripes, you will have drawn a lion!

3 For a leopard, change the colour of the face and add spots. Lose the shaggy fur around the chin.

Cool chameleon

Many chameleons change colour depending on their surroundings. Ours lives in the rainforest, so it's green. What colour will yours be? Will it have stripes or spots?

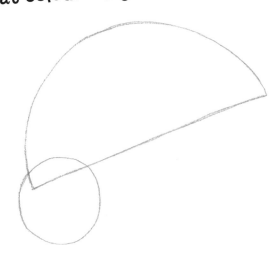

1 Start with a semicircle for the body. Draw it sloping at an angle to give the idea that the chameleon is sitting on a branch. Add a small circle for the curled-up tail.

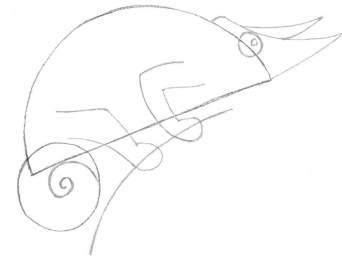

2 Next draw the legs, making sure they bend in different directions. Start the head by adding spiky horns and an eye. Draw the tail and a curved line for the branch.

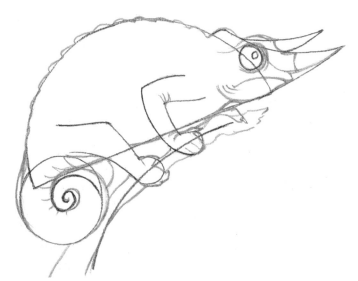

3 Add a zigzag outline to create a spiny back, and carefully copy the detail on the head, legs and tail. Don't be afraid to move away from the guidelines. Fill out the branch.

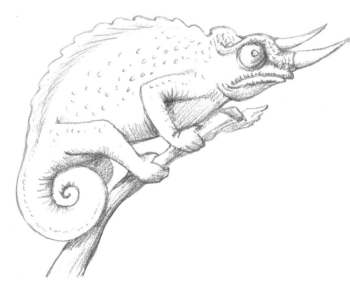

4 Rub out your basic shapes, then make the chameleon come alive with shading. Add tiny circles to give the skin texture and work on the detail of the feet and face.

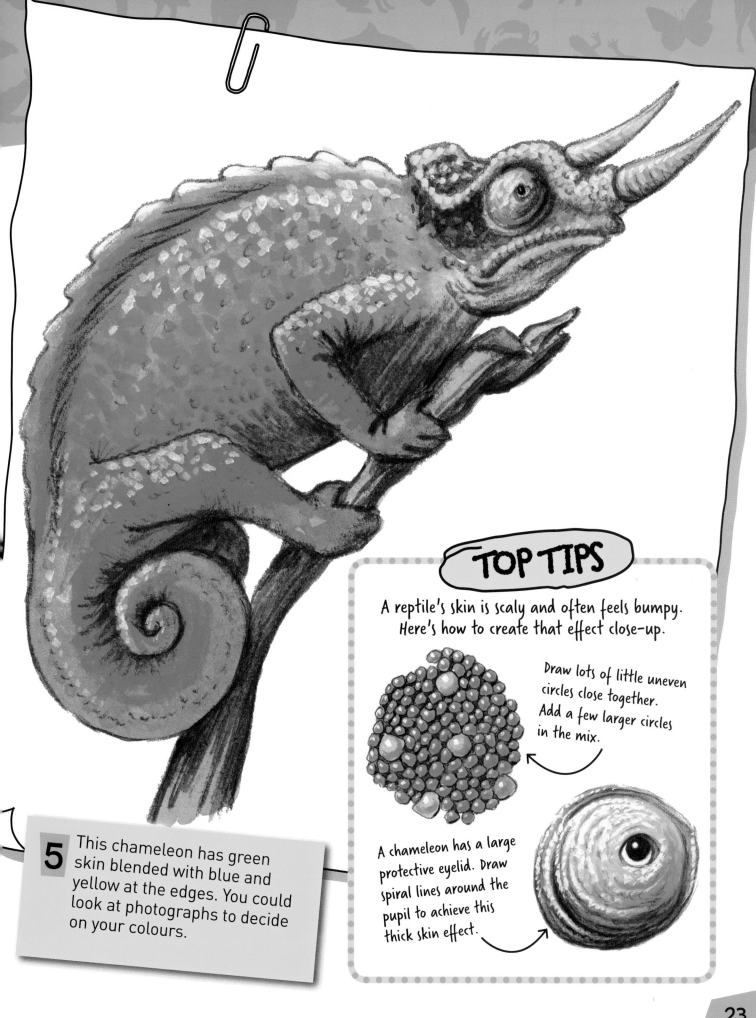

TOP TIPS

A reptile's skin is scaly and often feels bumpy. Here's how to create that effect close-up.

Draw lots of little uneven circles close together. Add a few larger circles in the mix.

A chameleon has a large protective eyelid. Draw spiral lines around the pupil to achieve this thick skin effect.

5 This chameleon has green skin blended with blue and yellow at the edges. You could look at photographs to decide on your colours.

23

Snappy crocodile

You wouldn't want a real-life croc snapping at your feet but this cartoon version is a lot more friendly! You can have him crawling along in just four simple steps.

1 Draw two ovals for the body and tail. With cartoon animals, it's a good idea to make the head quite big, so add a large triangular shape for this.

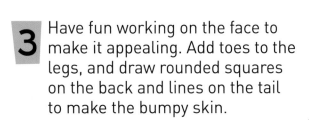

2 Next plot out the head with eyes and nostrils and a line for the snout. Add curves for the back and tail. Start to form the legs.

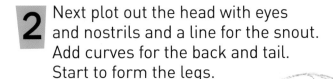

3 Have fun working on the face to make it appealing. Add toes to the legs, and draw rounded squares on the back and lines on the tail to make the bumpy skin.

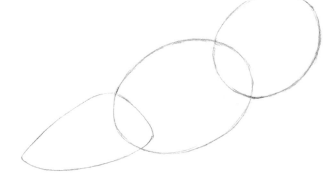

4 Before colouring in, go over the outlines with a black felt-tip pen. When it's dry, rub out your pencil lines.

CARTOON CORNER

Try out different expressions for your croc. Study yourself in the mirror pulling these faces first to help.

1

For an angry face, scrunch up the eyes and make the nostrils wide. Close most of the mouth but leave some teeth on show.

2

For a happy face, make the mouth wide and smiling with lots of teeth on show. The eyes should be wide open.

3

Use props to help. As well as drawing your croc licking his lips, add a knife, fork and napkin to make him look really hungry!

Leaping dolphin

To draw a dophin really well, it's important to capture its streamlined shape. Use smooth lines and keep the colour simple. In no time at all, it will be leaping off the page!

1 To draw the body, start with a banana shape. Add triangles for the fin, flipper and tail. Position them accurately.

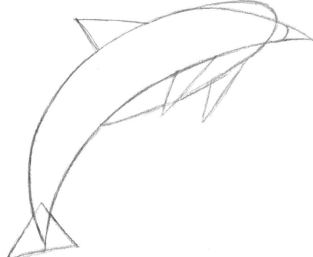

2 Draw a long, curved line around the front of the body to form the belly and head. Include another small curve for the nose and mouth. Draw the second flipper.

3 Give the fin, flippers and tail smooth, curved outlines. Work on the mouth so it shows a friendly smile. Add an eye.

4 Once the detail is complete, carefully rub out the basic shapes. You should be left with a sleek, streamlined sea animal.

TOP TIPS

Try drawing another leaping dolphin. Keep the basic body shape above but change the expression on its face. Here's how to draw a laughing dolphin!

Make sure that the mouth is open and rounded. Colour the inside pink to suggest a tongue. Add lots of small pointed teeth, evenly spaced apart.

5 Colour the dolphin in different shades of grey and add white highlights. Use firm strokes to keep the skin looking smooth.

Shark attack!

This cartoon shark looks scary and funny at the same time! When you're an expert at drawing him this way, try varying the length of his tail and the size of his teeth.

1 Start with an extra-large circle for the head. Then draw two curved lines that meet at a point for the body and tail.

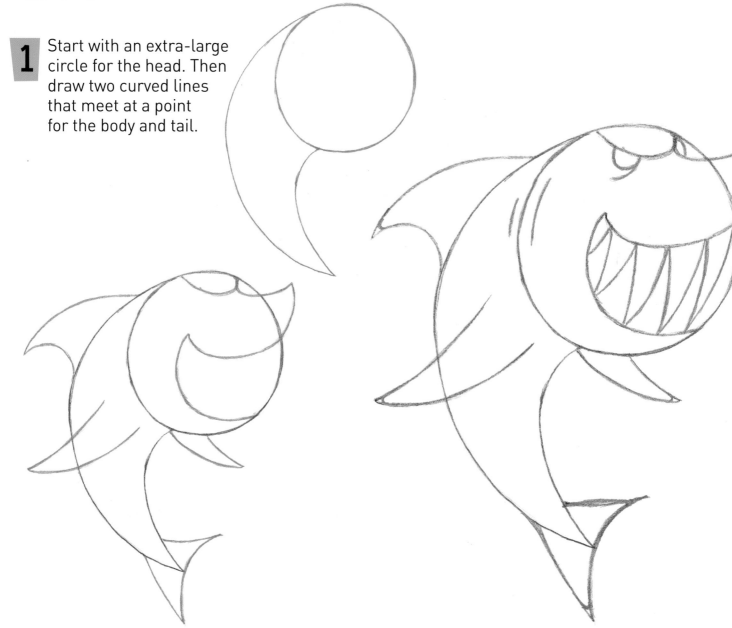

2 You can add movement by drawing more pointed curves for the fins and tail. Copy the picture carefully, especially the head and mouth.

3 Now draw the pointed teeth and scary eyes. Add three gill lines and round off the tips of the fins and tail. This will make the teeth look even sharper!

4 Rub out the circle around the head and colour your shark in two shades of blue. Give it pale yellow and white teeth.

CARTOON CORNER

Here are some tips for drawing other crazy cartoon fish.

1 As with the shark, start this goldfish with a circle and a pointed curve. Give it large wonky eyes and a lopsided mouth to make it look really silly. Add fine lines for the tail, fin and flippers.

2 To draw this tropical fish, use two overlapping triangles. Experiment with different angles and sizes. Try different colours too, and add wavy lines or stripes instead of spots.

Top toucan

For this picture, you're going to work with a set of boxes, or a grid, to draw a toucan from the side. When you draw animals or people side on, it is called a profile.

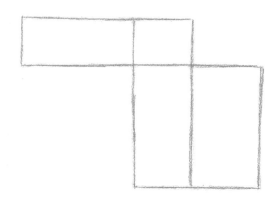

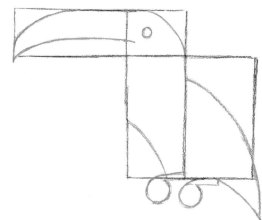

1 Carefully copy the grid above. You can use a ruler to help you make the lines straight and at right angles.

2 Work inside the boxes, drawing curves for the bill, head and body. Outside, add circles for the feet and curved, crossing lines to start the tail feathers. Don't forget the eye.

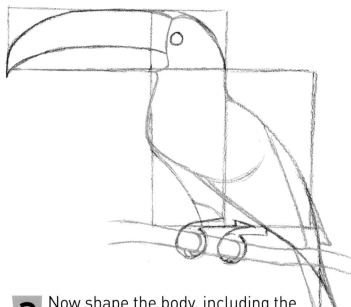

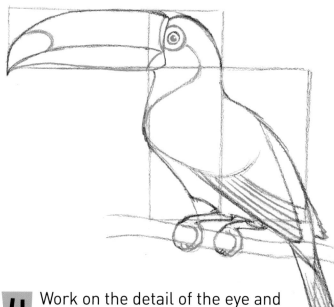

3 Now shape the body, including the triangular wings. Add a rectangle around the tail feather lines, and draw a branch between the feet.

4 Work on the detail of the eye and bill. Add evenly spaced lines for the feathers. Make the feet grip the branch, then rub out the grid.

TOP TIPS

A good artist always works hard on the details.
This will help make your pictures look more realistic.

Instead of using solid black, blend in deep blue and grey to show light catching the feathers.

Birds' feet are scaly so draw dark curved lines to bring this out. Study how the feet grip the branch.

31

Swooping owl

Have a go at capturing a brown owl swooping down from the sky. This time you're going to draw the whole outline first, so all the hard work is done up front!

1 Start by drawing a circle with a curved line down the middle for the head. Copy the torpedo-shaped body, then add wings and a squashed semicircle for the tail.

2 Next concentrate on the owl's face. Use the centre line as a guide for placing the beak and large eyes. Owls have feathered legs so make these thick and rounded.

3 Now work on the wing and tail feathers. Follow the outline carefully, making each feather shape even and about the same size. Then rub out the outlines.

4 Brown owls are dull in colour to allow them to hide easily, so use shades of brown and cream. Make the wing tips darker to help them stand out.

CARTOON CORNER

Here are some different shaped birds you can practise drawing.

1

2

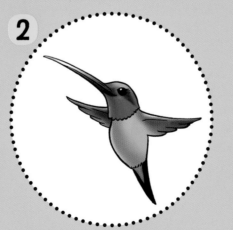

3

A mighty eagle has large black wings. Make its hooked beak and sharp talons stand out by colouring them bright yellow.

Tiny hummingbirds come in lots of colours. Give them long pointed beaks for drinking sweet nectar from flowers.

Draw a penguin as if it's wearing a black jacket and give it a rounded white belly. Notice how its webbed feet are quite large.

Darting dragonfly

Dragonflies - with their lacy wings and pencil-thin bodies - are one of the fastest flying insects in the world. Follow the steps to draw a beautiful dragonfly about to land.

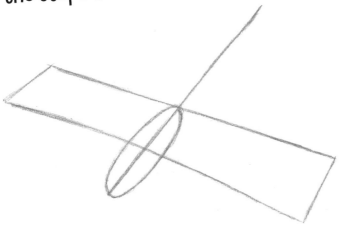

1 For this first step, look closely at the angles. Draw a straight angled line for the body, then add a rectangle for the wings. An oval forms the upper body and head.

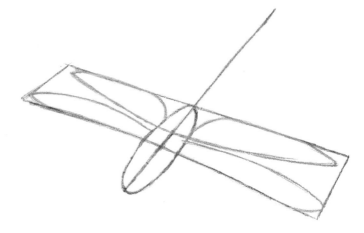

2 Now draw the four long, curved wings neatly inside the rectangle. Notice that the back wings are a little shorter and thicker than the front wings.

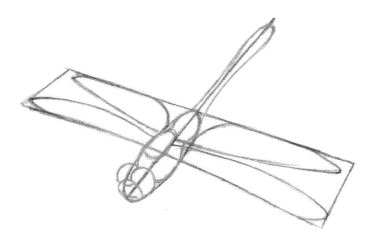

3 Following the guideline, draw the body. Make the upper body thicker than the rest. Copy the head, making sure that you have drawn two huge eyes.

4 Carefully rub out the guidelines and add the thin bent legs and feet. To make the lower body rounded, draw curved lines. Develop the shape of the lower wings.

5 Go over the outline with a fine black felt-tip pen before you colour it in. Leave gaps along the wings to make them look transparent. Add detail to the wings and hairs on the front legs.

TOP TIPS

When you get the chance, watch insects in the wild. Looking at a real dragonfly close-up can help you to draw it accurately.

A dragonfly's huge eyes allow it to see in many directions at once. Copy them closely. Notice the fine hairs around the mouth as well.

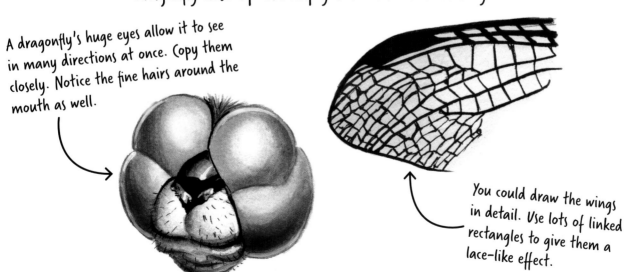

You could draw the wings in detail. Use lots of linked rectangles to give them a lace-like effect.

The next step

BY THE POND

Remember the dragonfly (pages 34-5) and horse (pages 18-19) you drew? How about making them part of a beautiful pond scene on a summer's day?

In a scene like this, your racehorse will need to be much smaller.

Make the sky a lighter blue as it fades into the distance. Work with a horizon line to divide the land from the sky.

Allow the leafy background to show through the dragonfly's wings to make them look almost see-through.

Draw the reflection of a tree upside down using wavy lines to create a sense of movement in the water.

When you draw plants and flowers, think about their shape as well as their colour.

If you add a green shadow beneath the dragonfly, it will make it look like it is really standing on the leaf.

PEOPLE

Being able to draw people is a real challenge but all it takes is practice. In this section, you'll find lots of tips for drawing life-like people and expressive cartoon characters.

Figures

Discover how to get heads and bodies in proportion to make your drawings super-realistic.

Expressions

Bring a fun cartoon character to life with different expressions.

Clothing

Practise drawing clothes and capturing a pose for a fashion model.

Action!

Get to grips with creating excitement and action when you draw this skater boy performing a trick.

Movement

Find out how to set your characters in motion.

Figures

When drawing a human figure, you need to get the proportions right - that's the size of their head, bodies, arms and legs in relation to one another. A grid can help you with this.

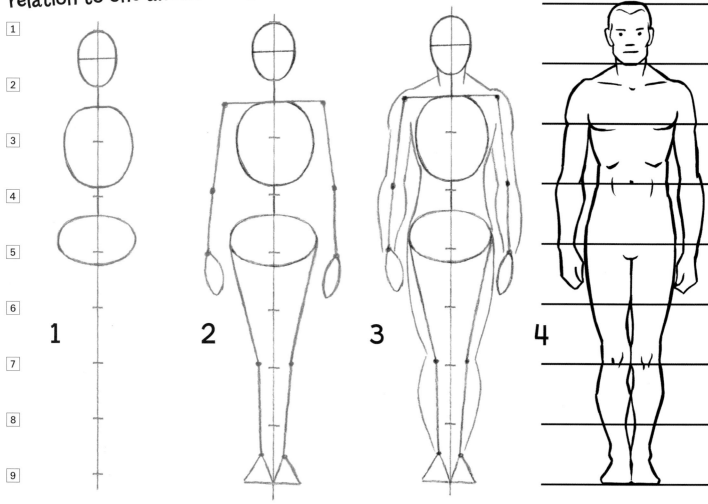

1 2 3 4

1 Draw a grid with nine marks, each one the same distance apart. Add an oval for the head between the first two marks and draw a horizontal line across the middle. Draw more ovals between marks 2 and 6.

2 Form the shoulders with a straight line and draw stick arms and legs. Use the grid to get the lengths right. Mark the joints with dots. Then draw simple shapes for the hands and feet.

3 Now flesh out your skeleton with an outline. Notice how the outline nips in around the joints but bulges elsewhere to create a muscular body.

4 Rub out your basic shapes and add definition to the body with curved lines. Then fill in the face. Here, you can clearly see the man's height against the grid.

5 This figure is wearing a T-shirt and jeans but you can give your person any clothes you like. These simple clothes follow the figure's outline. Try adding bigger, bulkier clothes to change the shape of the body.

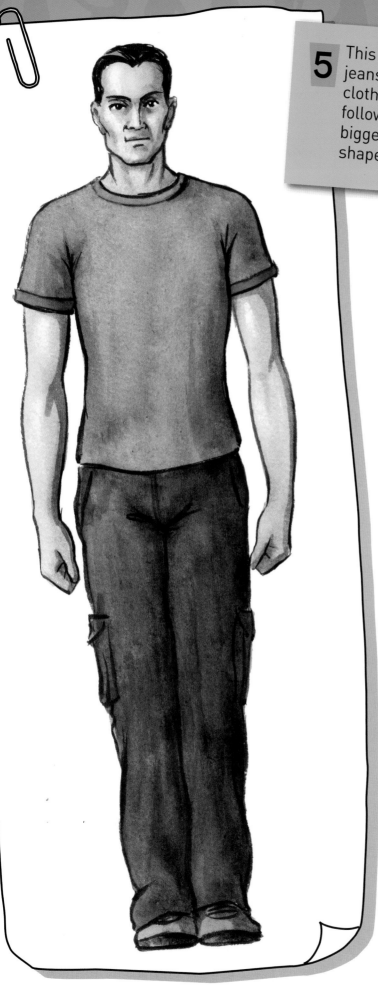

TOP TIPS

Draw children so that they have a larger head in relation to their bodies. This young boy stands about six heads high. A toddler would be about four heads high.

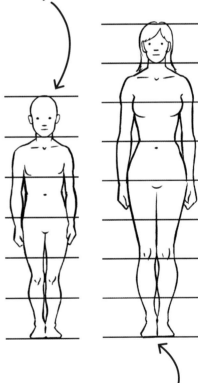

You can use the same basic skeleton for drawing a female as you did for the man. But make the shoulders and chest narrower, and the legs and arms more curvy in shape.

Poses

Here you're going to use body language and pose to convey a mood. Take a look at this grumpy teacher – you wouldn't want to mess with her!

1 Start with three ovals for the head, chest and wide hips. Overlapping the shapes will help to make the cartoon figure look old and hunched. Don't forget to include the face guides.

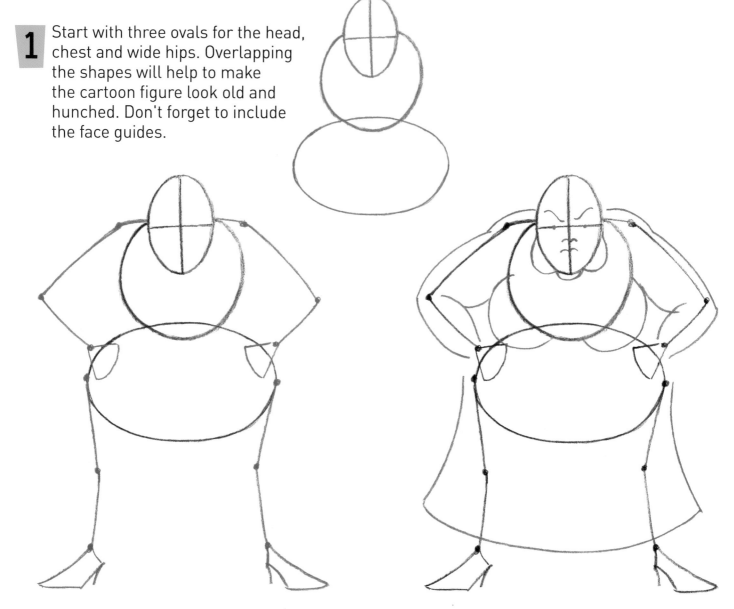

2 Now add the shoulders and arms. Follow the angles carefully so that the hands can sit on the hips. Draw stick legs and mark the joints. Make the shoes really pointy.

3 Finally, give your teacher her bulging shape. Work on her rounded arms and chest. Add a collar for her shirt and a long wide skirt. Finish off the her legs and create a frightful face.

4 When designing costumes and hairstyles, look at pictures to help you. This grumpy teacher has a bun, round glasses and old-fashioned clothes in drab colours.

CARTOON CORNER

Work on different poses and body language to get a mood across!

1

This figure, with its folded arms, doesn't want to do what you're asking.

2

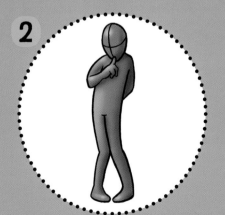

To make a character look shy, give it knocked knees and pigeon toes.

3

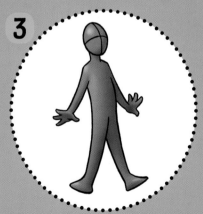

With its legs apart and open hands, this character seems really shocked.

Faces

To draw a realistic face well, you need to pay attention to the details. Once you've mastered this face, how about getting a family member to sit for you while you paint their portrait?

1 Draw an egg shape. Then add guidelines down and across the middle. Mark four equally spaced points on the horizontal line. In the lower half of the face draw lines for the nose and mouth.

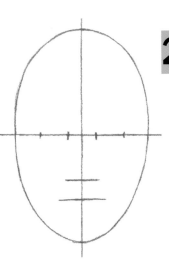

2 Copy the position of the eyes, carefully following the horizontal guide, then draw two lines down to the nose. Add the ears, eyebrows and mouth shape. Start to form the slender neck.

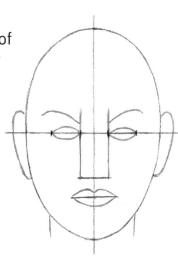

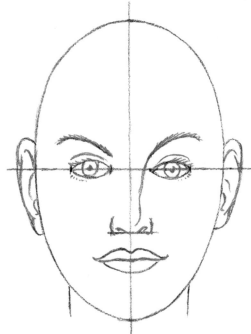

3 With the guides in place, you can now work on the details. Look in the mirror or at faces in magazines to get a feel for the shapes of different types of features.

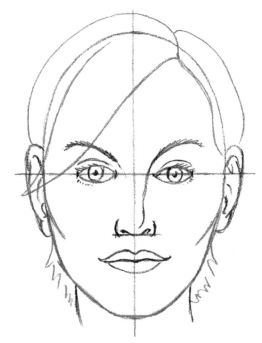

4 When working on the hair, think about the overall shape. Remember that hair has thickness and stands out from the head. Finally, touch up the face, paying attention to the jawline and cheekbones.

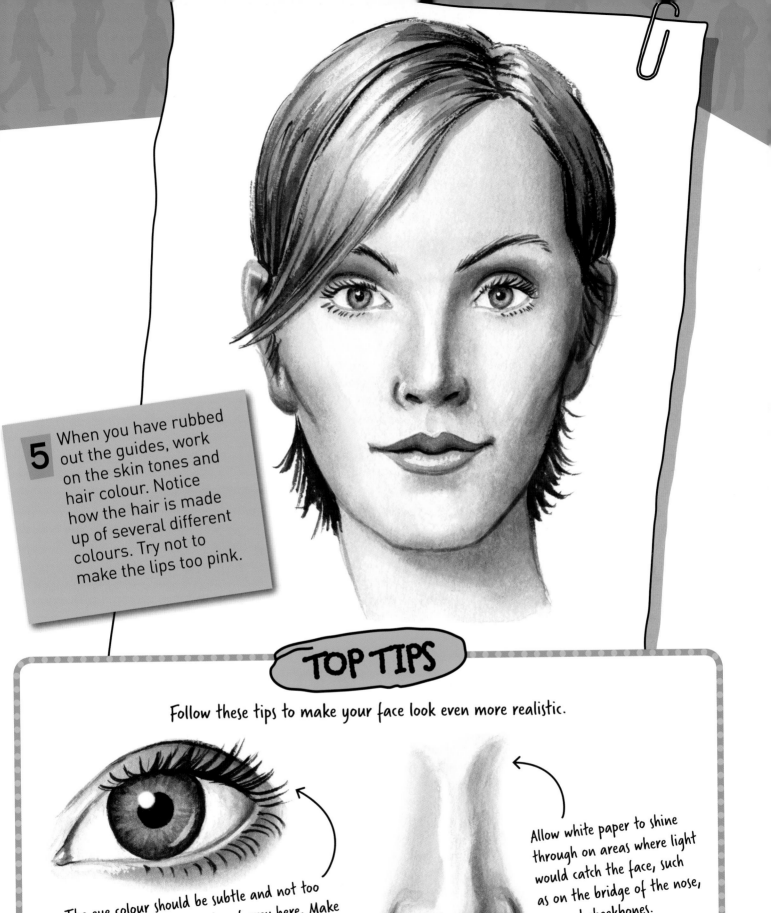

5 When you have rubbed out the guides, work on the skin tones and hair colour. Notice how the hair is made up of several different colours. Try not to make the lips too pink.

TOP TIPS

Follow these tips to make your face look even more realistic.

The eye colour should be subtle and not too bright. We have used shades of grey here. Make sure that the eyelashes are well defined.

Allow white paper to shine through on areas where light would catch the face, such as on the bridge of the nose, lips and cheekbones.

Expressions

The best way to bring a character to life is by giving it an engaging expression, as in the case of this laughing boy. Let the expression shape the face rather than the other way round.

1 Start with a simple circle and add curved guidelines to make the face point upwards. Use the guides to position the squinting eyes and the huge mouth.

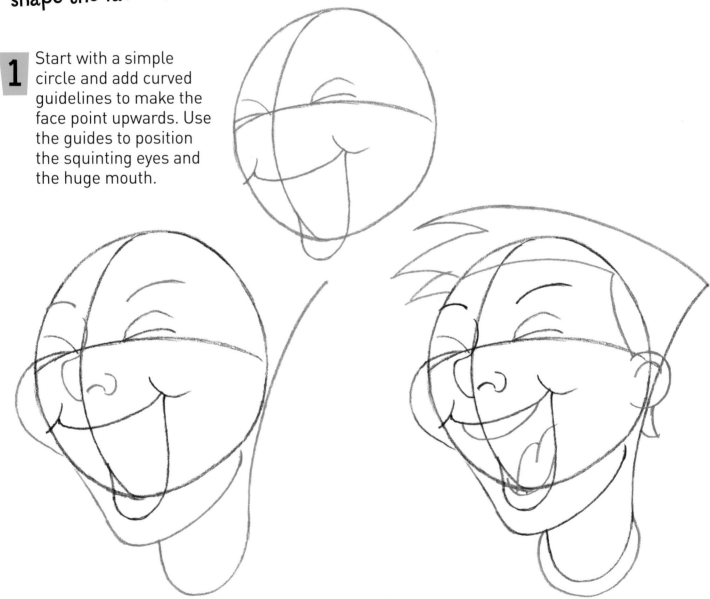

2 Emphasize the laughing expression by shaping the long jawline and the bulging cheek. Then add the nose and the eyebrows. Create the neck and back of the hair with a long sweeping line.

3 Work on the mouth further by drawing lips, teeth and a tongue. Shape the spiky quiffed hair with jagged strokes and draw the ear. Finish off with a curved neckline, then rub out your guides.

4 Keep your cartoon character bright and simple in colour. This boy has black hair but yours could have brown, fair or red hair. Notice how his cheeks are highlighted so they stand out.

CARTOON CORNER

It doesn't take too much work to change your laughing boy into a crying one!

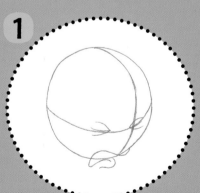

1 Draw a circle as before but add guidelines to make the face point downwards. Keep the squinting eyes and make the mouth smaller.

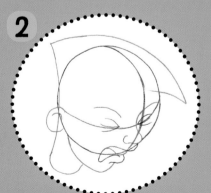

2 You need a long chin but no bulging cheek this time. The quiff, nose and eyebrows are similar to before yet your picture looks different!

3 Colour in the boy then add some flying tears. This is an artist's trick to make the character look like he is crying rather than in pain.

Clothing

When you draw this graceful fashion model, spend lots of time developing her clothing. Don't forget that clothes can really give a character their personality.

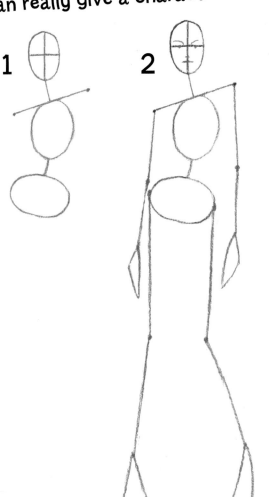  

1 Draw three ovals for the head, chest and body. Add an angled line for the movement of her shoulders and give her a long neck. Draw the face guides.

2 When you add the stick arms and legs, remember how tall catwalk models are. Shape the hands and feet, then position the facial features.

3 Although much of the model's body will be covered up, it is still worth drawing an outline to make her seem real and to develop her pose. Shape her hair too.

4 Now add the clothes and boots. Make her thick jacket sit well away from her slim arms. Give her dress movement by drawing flowing lines on the skirt.

5 When adding the final touches, work swiftly and use smooth lines. Do the same when you colour in – try to cover the paper with as few strokes as possible. This is how real fashion illustrators work!

TOP TIPS

When drawing and colouring clothing, try to capture the texture of the different materials.

Use bold dark lines and bright highlights for the shiny leather. In contrast, make the sheepskin soft and fluffy wih a broken outline.

Although these boots are also made of leather, they have a matt look. Blend the colours gently and add almost no highlights to the top of the boot.

Movement

The tricky thing to achieve in this cartoon drawing is the twist as the girl runs. But if you follow the steps carefully you'll soon have her sprinting off in all directions!

1 Copy the stick drawing, concentrating on the angles of the lines and the different shapes. Notice how large the head is and also how the shoulder line cuts across the chest.

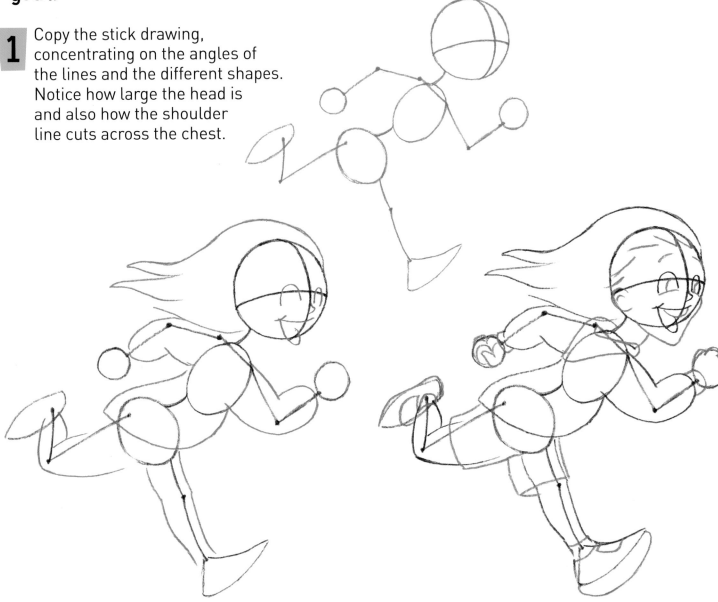

2 There is no need to draw the full body outline, so work on the baggy top instead. Outline the legs and shape the hair making sure it flows back. Position the facial features including the open mouth.

3 Develop the face further, paying attention to the jawline. Work on the hands, then finish off the trainers and the clothing. The position of the hood makes it clear that her shoulders are turning away.

4 Once you have rubbed out the guides, go over the outline with a dark felt-tip pen and colour in. To turn the girl into a boy, simply shorten the hair, lose the long eyelashes and change the colour scheme.

CARTOON CORNER

Motion lines create the illusion of speed. Check out these tips for drawing different types of lines.

1

2

3

Create a sense of movement in the arms and legs with short curved lines. Draw a ground line to show how the girl's feet are in the air.

To give the sense that your character is speeding forwards, draw straight lines behind her. Add long curves by the arm to show it lifting up.

This time the girl is racing by in a blur! Draw a smoke trail behind her, angle lines upwards and blend her bottom half into a spiral of colour.

49

Balance

Try drawing an elegant ballerina in this graceful pose, then find pictures of other dance positions to copy. You could even show a whole ballet sequence step by step.

1 Draw three ovals linked by a curved line. Leave plenty of space between the shapes to keep the body looking slender. Make the head small and include the face guide.

2 Now work on the legs and arms. These need to be long and stretched out. Shape the hands and feet so they are fully extended too. Make sure your stick drawing looks balanced.

3 As you outline the body, make the lines flow so that the figure looks graceful. Don't make the ballerina too skinny – you need strong muscles to hold a pose like this!

4 Spend time on the hands and feet so they appear delicate. Then draw simple swirls for the ballet dress. Take care with the dancer's expression so that everything looks effortless.

5 When you finish off the dress and outline the body, work with a fine brush in dark pink to avoid harsh lines. Notice the tiny shadow, which connects her with the floor and shows you she is holding a pose rather than leaping.

TOP TIPS

A ballerina needs a graceful hair-do and the right kind of pumps. Here's how to draw and colour them.

A neat bun makes the perfect hairstyle. Draw the overall shape first. Then use fine brushes or pencils in shades of brown to create the hair strands.

Work with different shades of pink for the ballet pumps and give them white highlights. Notice that she's wearing pink tights as well. This creates a delicate and subtle look.

Action!

You can have lots of fun with this cartoon skateboarder. Draw him performing this trick, then experiment with his clothing and the designs on his board.

1 In this picture, you are looking up at the skater boy so the soles of his feet are on view. Copy the drawing carefully to get the position of the skeleton just right.

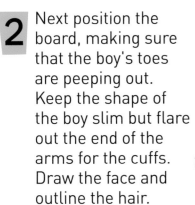

2 Next position the board, making sure that the boy's toes are peeping out. Keep the shape of the boy slim but flare out the end of the arms for the cuffs. Draw the face and outline the hair.

3 Finally work on the details. Add texture to the hair, develop the face and shape the fingers. Draw the baggy shorts and give the skateboard its wheels. Rub out the guides.

4 Skateboarders often wear bold colours and like dramatic designs. This boy has a flame design on his board and a T-shirt to match. Instead of the skull motif, you could draw more flames.

CARTOON CORNER

Why not have a go at creating some different sporty characters?

1

Copy the pose for this footballer carefully, noticing how his arms are outstretched, his back leg is bent and that he is looking down towards the ball. Choose a colour scheme for his kit and add motion lines.

2

The pose of this tennis player is quite different. She has her arms raised and is looking up towards the ball to give the idea that she is about to serve. Her flying pigtails add to the effect but you can give her any hairstyle.

Perfect hands

If you want to make a human figure look really convincing, then you need to get the hands right. Here we show you how to draw hands in different positions.

Clenched fist

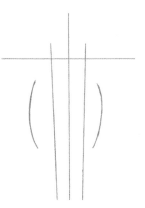

1 When a hand grips an object, it's best to start with the object first, in this case a sword. Copy the drawing to position the sword and mark the edges of the fist.

2 Next draw the top and bottom of the fist using the curves as a guide. Mark on the fingers and thumb, and a curve for the knuckles. Start adding details to the sword

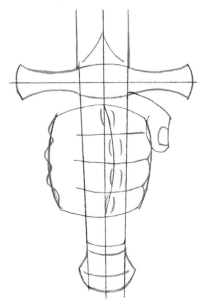

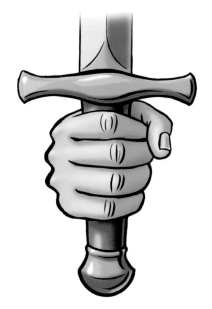

3 Draw the wavy outlines that end the fist and add detail to the knuckles. Give the thumb its fingernail. Shape the sword's handle and blade, then rub out the guides.

4 To create realistic skin tones, use pale pink and blend it with a little yellow. Add a touch of purple for the darker areas. Leave the knuckles pale for highlights.

Open hand

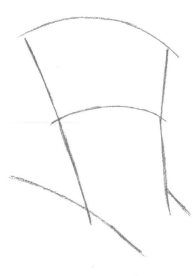 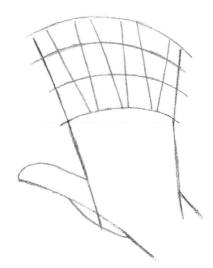 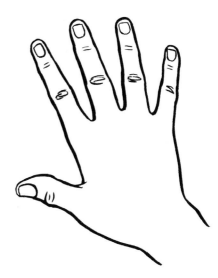

1 This open hand is almost a fan shape. Start with the bottom half and mark on lines for the thumb and wrist. Then add two guide-lines with a curve on top for placing the fingers.

2 With the fingers, it's easiest to draw three wedge shapes first. Mark the curves for the knuckles, then shape the thumb and fleshy part underneath.

3 When going over the outline, remember that the fingers should bulge slightly at the knuckles. Carefully draw on the fingernails and add small crease lines for the joints.

Pointing hand

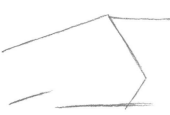 

1 Shape the ball of the hand first, making sure that the bottom part where the thumb will be is flat. Add a short line to mark the wrist and a long line for the pointing finger.

2 Now add shape to the fingers. Lightly curve the pointing finger and make the bottom of the thumb fleshy. Mark a cross above the thumb for the hidden clenched fingers.

3 Press hard with your pencil to give the pointing hand a strong outline and make it look solid. Press lightly to create the finer creases. Don't forget to include the nails.

The next step

IN THE PLAYGROUND

Try using the grumpy teacher (pages 40-1), the running girl (pages 48-9) and the skater boy (pages 52-3) to create an action-packed cartoon playground scene.

Pick up the colour of the sky in the windows to give them a sense of reflection.

By overlapping the main characters, you tie the action together.

Include background details such as trees and houses to make the playground seem real.

Drawing shadows underneath the characters helps make them appear off the ground and on the move.

Make sure the motion lines stand out against the dark playground.

Add colourful playground markings leading into the action to draw in your eye.

MONSTERS

In this section, it's time to get creative! You'll discover how to draw classic beasts but you can also use your imagination to give them a twist of your own.

Werewolf
Find out how to make a monster look truly wild when you draw this crazed werewolf.

Crazy creature
Experiment with colour and shape to create different cartoon creatures.

Sea serpent
Think about colour combinations when you bring this angry sea serpent to life.

Zombie
Look out for tips on how to draw a scary zombie face.

Yeti
Turn a terrifying legendary monster into an almost cuddly cartoon beast.

Scary werewolf

A werewolf is half-man and half-beast so he needs ferocious features and a wild expression. Dramatic, dark colours will help to make him look even more terrifying.

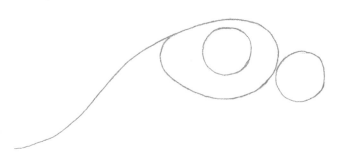

1 Draw an egg shape on its side with a long sweeping curve for the werewolf's back and tail. Place one small circle inside the egg and then another one just outside.

2 Now work on the hips and legs. Copy the drawing carefully, noticing the angle of the joints and the extra long feet. Don't forget the curved line for the arm.

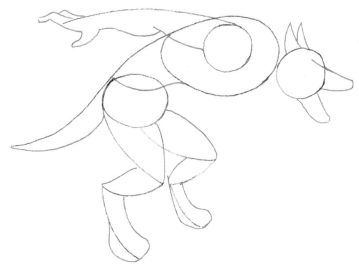

3 Give the werewolf its shape, making sure the feet are long and wide at the ends. Work carefully on the hand. Then draw the massive jaws and pointed ears.

4 Finally, give the werewolf its rough fur by drawing lots of jagged lines. Finish off the face, including the sharp teeth, and add the curved claws. Draw its ragged jeans.

5 To create the dramatic purple-grey fur, blend blue, red and brown. Contrast this with yellow-green eyes and dirty orange claws.

TOP TIPS

Check out these tips to make your werewolf look even more realistic and scary!

Work with an old scratchy paintbrush to create coarse, wiry fur. Add white highlights to make the gnarled fingers and claws stand out.

Notice how the teeth are curved as well as pointed. Paint them dirty yellow, not white, to make them look really mean!

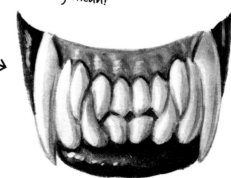

Crazy creature

Have a go at creating this colourful comic-book monster. Then let your imagination run riot and make up some more of your own!

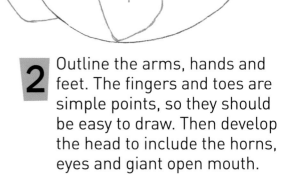

1 Start with a series of curves for the fat body and long neck. Notice how the neck lines curve the opposite way to the body for a cheeky twist of the head. Mark on two lines for the arms.

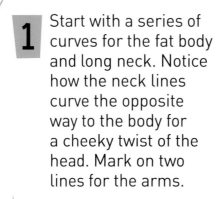

2 Outline the arms, hands and feet. The fingers and toes are simple points, so they should be easy to draw. Then develop the head to include the horns, eyes and giant open mouth.

3 The last step is to give your comic-book creation personality. Work on the buck teeth and wriggling tongue, then outline the lips. Draw thick eyebrows and bat-like ears. Don't forget to finish off the tail.

4 A cheerful character like this needs to be colourful! Create a rainbow effect by blending purple into red, orange and yellow, or choose your own colours.

CARTOON CORNER

Create some more funny monsters by starting with simple shapes.

1

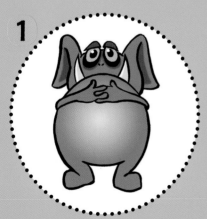

Draw a circle to shape this purple poppet's big fat belly.

2

A triangle forms the body of this green-eyed monster.

3

Start with a diamond for this monster, then add a huge mouth and flat feet.

Alien invasion

Aliens could come in all shapes and sizes but with its huge eyes and humanoid shape, this is a classic type. Follow the steps to draw a picture from a different world.

1 This figure almost looks like it's upside down, but it's not! The circle for the head needs to be bigger than those for the body. Join the circles with a line.

2 Now draw the arms and legs. Make the lines straight and pay attention to the angles. Different-sized circles form the hands and the feet are diamond shapes.

3 Outline the body, keeping it thin but muscly-looking. Draw curved lines for the long, bendy fingers and add guidelines to the head to help you draw the features. Shape the chin.

4 It's important to get the face detail right, this is what makes your alien come alive. Copy the picture and carefully follow the grid. Then shape the fingers and rub out the guides.

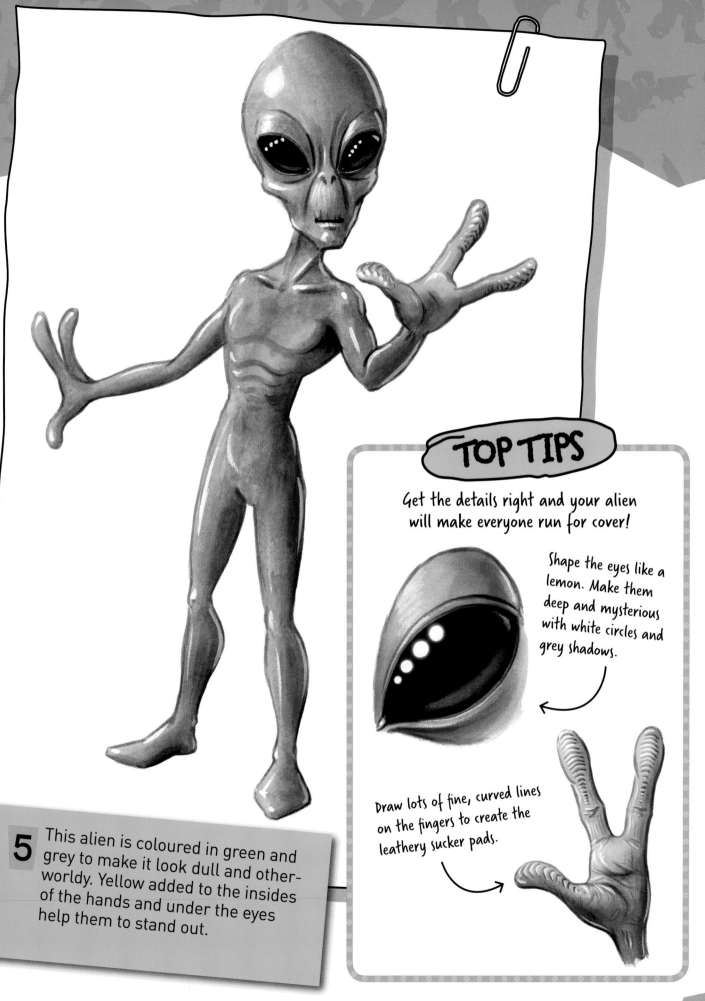

TOP TIPS

Get the details right and your alien will make everyone run for cover!

Shape the eyes like a lemon. Make them deep and mysterious with white circles and grey shadows.

Draw lots of fine, curved lines on the fingers to create the leathery sucker pads.

5 This alien is coloured in green and grey to make it look dull and other-worldy. Yellow added to the insides of the hands and under the eyes help them to stand out.

MONSTERS
Ancient mummy

Yikes - it's a mummy on the loose! This is a fairly simple cartoon drawing so you should have this bandaged horror walking off the page in no time at all.

1 First draw a circle for the head and a sausage shape for the body. Then draw two banana shapes for the outstretched arms and lines for the legs.

2 Make the hands wide and the thumbs fat. Shape the legs, remembering that they should seem fairly stiff, and add large feet.

3 Now work on the bandages. Follow the picture carefully, noticing that some lines curve up and some down. This will help to make your drawing look three-dimensional. Finally add the face.

4 Outline the bandages with a black felt-tip pen and colour them pale yellow-brown. Add darker shading to make them look old and worn.

CARTOON CORNER

The Egyptians also mummified their cats. Learn how to draw this one to keep your mummy company.

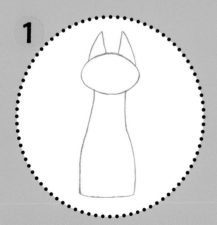

1

Draw a bottle shape for the body and an oval for the head. Add two ears.

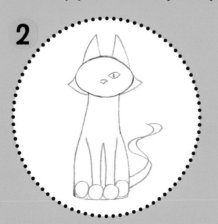

2

Now shape the legs, paws and tail. Notice the cat only has one eye!

3

Finish the bandages in the same way as before. Add a loose one like a tail.

Sea serpent

Is it a snake? Is it a dragon? No, it's a seriously scary sea serpent! Most of the detail is in the monster's head so take time over this part and your picture will spring into life.

1 Start with two different-sized circles. Then draw two swooping curved lines to join the circles together. You should now have a looping worm-like shape.

2 Continue the end of the front loop. Then do the same at the back, but make it thinner and taper it into a point. You have created your sea serpent's long body and tail.

3 Now draw guidelines for the head and the fins that will run along the length of the body. Add two jointed lines for the long legs and wide feet.

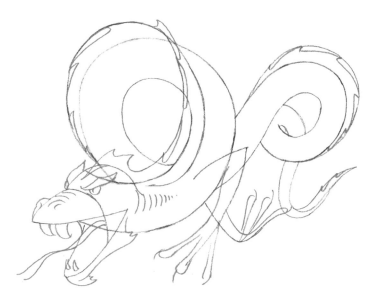

4 Follow the guidelines along the monster's back to draw the fins. Then finish off the legs and feet. Add detail to the neck and face including the teeth and forked tongue.

5 You can make your sea serpent any colour but blue and green work well for a watery feel. Paint more faintly towards the tail to suggest depth and distance.

TOP TIPS

A forked tongue and webbed feet are striking features. It pays to draw and colour them well.

Follow the shape of the curves here carefully. Make the back of the tongue dark green and contrast it with pink to make the forked part stand out.

Add white highlights to the feet to give them texture and make them seem scaly. Use a different shade of green for the webbing.

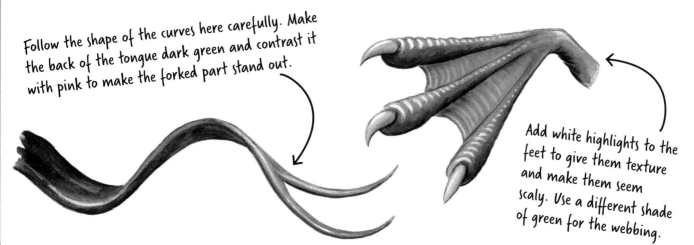

Dramatic dragon

Don't get too close to this dangerous dragon! His classic features include scalloped wings and an arrow tail, but you could experiment with drawing giant horns and spines as well.

1 Draw an egg shape for the chest. Then add curved lines for the haunches and tail. Another curve with a triangle on top forms the head.

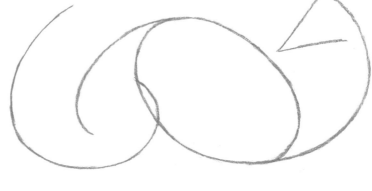

2 Now carefully outline the head and the neck. Start the legs, making sure they bend and point forwards. Shape the tail and begin the wings.

3 A dragon's wings are a bit like bats' wings and its feet like those of an eagle. Copy the picture to get them right. Work on the detail of the face and add the arrow to the top of the tail.

4 Your dragon doesn't have to be green! This one is brown, orange and purple. You could also give it stripes or patches instead of spots.

CARTOON CORNER

Why not try drawing a fire-breathing baby dragon and show him standing up?

1

Start with a small circle for the head and taper it into a muzzle. For the body, draw a pear shape. Then add the tail.

2

Work on the arms, legs and head. To keep the baby dragon looking cute, make sure all the lines are curved or rounded.

3

Add a few spikes to the finished drawing and a puff of flames from his mouth. Keep the outline smooth and the colours simple.

Zombie horror

When you draw this zombie, remember that it is a lifeless corpse that has risen from the dead! Make its features hideous and give it grey, decaying flesh.

1 Draw three ovals for the head, chest and hips. Copy the shapes and their positions accurately, then join them up with a line.

2 Next add a long, bent line for the sloping shoulders. Draw more lines for the legs and shape the feet. Mark the guides on the head. Your stick figure should already look zombie-like.

3 Bring your zombie to life by working on the straggly hair and face. When outlining the body, make the clothes look ragged.

4 When drawing the hands and feet, remember that zombies are often skinny and their joints gnarled. Fill in the face and finish off the clothing. Then rub out the guides.

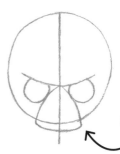

Mark guidelines on the head. Then draw the skull-like eye sockets and upper jaw.

Now outline the shape of the lower jaw and develop the eyes and nose. Widen the cheeks.

Contrast the sickly-looking skin with red eyes and yellow teeth. Add lines to make the face seem even more ghoulish and make the hair scruffy.

5 A ghastly zombie needs a ghastly paintbrush, so dig out the oldest, scruffiest one you can find! Use yucky browns and a dash of acid green for a grimy and toxic look.

Hairy yeti

A cuddly cartoon yeti is fairly simple to draw. We're not sure if you'd really want to meet this legendary beast though. Ape-like yetis are rumoured to be enormous!

1 Start with two wonky egg shapes, one inside the other. They will form the yeti's arms and chest. Look at the picture carefully to get the shapes just right.

2 Next position the head. To do this, draw a circle with an overlapping oval. Shape the bottom of the arms and the yeti's legs and feet.

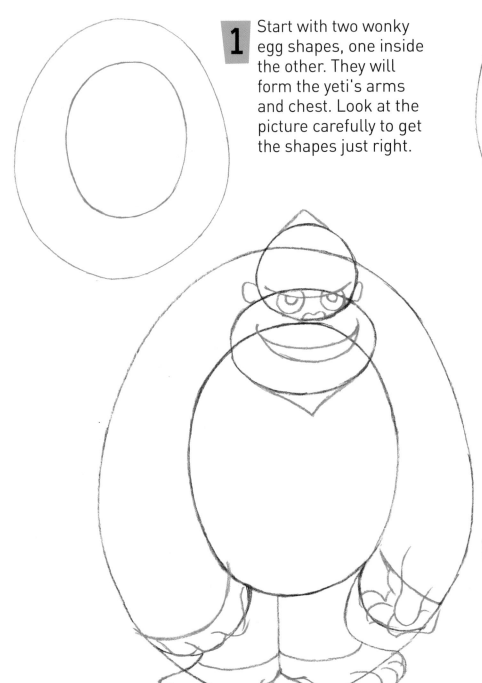

3 Give the creature a heavy brow and a smiling mouth. Make his chin pointed and don't forget the eyes. Notice that he has fewer fingers and toes than we do. This makes him even easier to draw! Rub out the guides.

4 When outlining the fur, use lots of thin lines. This will make your yeti look really hairy. Remember to draw his teeth. Colour him simply in pale blues contrasted with purple.

CARTOON CORNER

Follow the steps to draw this picture of a mischievous baby yeti.

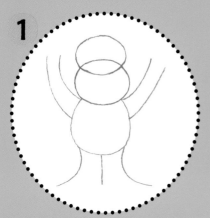

1 Draw a big head, round body and waving arms. Make the feet wide.

2 Then work on the fingers and toes as you did before. Fill in the face too.

3 Brighter colours and baby teeth make this little yeti a cuddly ball of fun!

The next step

NIGHT HORRORS

Bring your werewolf (pages 58-9) and zombie (pages 70-1) together out on the moor. Work with murky, dark colours to create this truly spooky moonlit scene.

Colour the sky a darker blue further away from the moon.

Make the moon large and round with shadows around it.

Your werewolf is in the background so keep it fairly small.

Leave some areas empty to add to the eerie feel.

Place your main zombie in the centre and make him large so he appears in the foreground, leaping out at you.

Include blue-white highlights to give contrast to the scene and make it look dramatic.

FANTASY CHARACTERS

Do you have a favourite fantasy hero or villain? Here are just a few of ours! Once you've mastered these creations, why not try to draw some of your own?

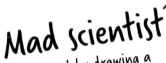

Superhero
Take your pick from a masked supergirl or a flying caped crusader.

Vampire
Follow the steps to bring a vile vampire back to life!

Mad scientist
Experiment by drawing a crazy cartoon scientist with an enormous head.

Evil orc
It's all about shape and texture with this evil orc.

Elf princess
Get creative with colour when you conjure up this woodland elf.

Girl power

Get ready for action and sketch this female superhero! With a superhero, the secret is to exaggerate the proportions of a human figure. Follow the steps to find out how.

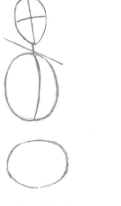

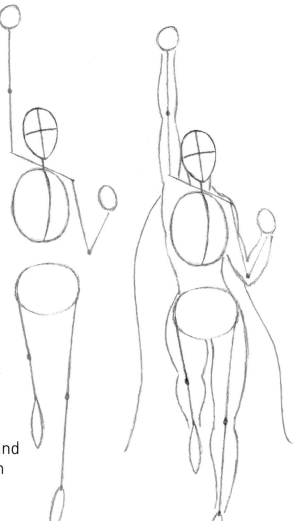

1 Start with three ovals for the head, chest and hips. Copy the picture carefully. Mark guidelines on the face and chest. Then add a sloping line for the shoulders.

2 Next draw stick legs and arms, paying attention to where they bend. Include dots for the joints. Notice how the front, raised leg is drawn shorter than the other one. The hands and feet can be oval shapes.

3 Outline the body using slightly curved lines to suggest powerful muscles. Narrow the lines at the joints. Then start to shape the cape.

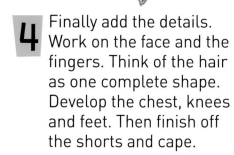

4 Finally add the details. Work on the face and the fingers. Think of the hair as one complete shape. Develop the chest, knees and feet. Then finish off the shorts and cape.

5 It's a good idea to keep to two or three contrasting colours for the colour scheme to create a dramatic effect. You could show your heroine without a mask or customize her accessories.

TOP TIPS

Drawing hands is a challenge, so take your time. You'll find more tips on pages 54–5.

First work on the basic clenched fist shape. Include lines for where the fingers and palm meet.

Now develop the fingers. Keep the shapes even. Notice how the thumb bulges at the joints.

When going over the outlines, add more shape to each knuckle. Crease marks on the palm will help to make the fist look tightly curled.

FANTASY CHARACTERS
Superhero

In this cartoon drawing, you're going to make the details in the foreground bigger so it looks like your action hero is flying off the page straight towards you.

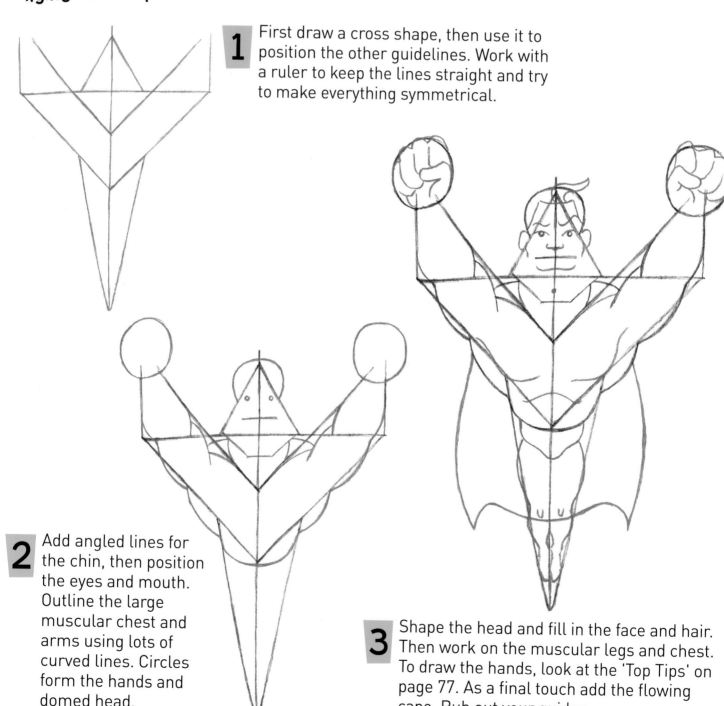

1 First draw a cross shape, then use it to position the other guidelines. Work with a ruler to keep the lines straight and try to make everything symmetrical.

2 Add angled lines for the chin, then position the eyes and mouth. Outline the large muscular chest and arms using lots of curved lines. Circles form the hands and domed head.

3 Shape the head and fill in the face and hair. Then work on the muscular legs and chest. To draw the hands, look at the 'Top Tips' on page 77. As a final touch add the flowing cape. Rub out your guides.

4 For this powerful character, use a thick black outline. Make it heavier around the head and arms and finer at the feet, so they look like they are farther away.

CARTOON CORNER

Now try drawing these mini superheroes, or invent your own!

1

2

3

What special powers do you think this colourful superboy has?

Big hair, stripes and a giant eye make this all-action girl stand out.

A green face and yellow eyes will make your character look wicked!

Vile vampire

Watch out for this bloodsucking vampire - he's not the friendly kind! Give him a deathly-pale face and a swishing blood-red cape to make him seem really creepy.

1 Start with two long curves to capture the vampire's overall pose and position of his legs. Mark a line for his shoulders. Then draw the head and add the guides.

2 Shape the long legs and feet. The arms and hands can be stick lines ending in ovals at this stage. Form the cape with a straight line from the arm and a broad curve at the bottom.

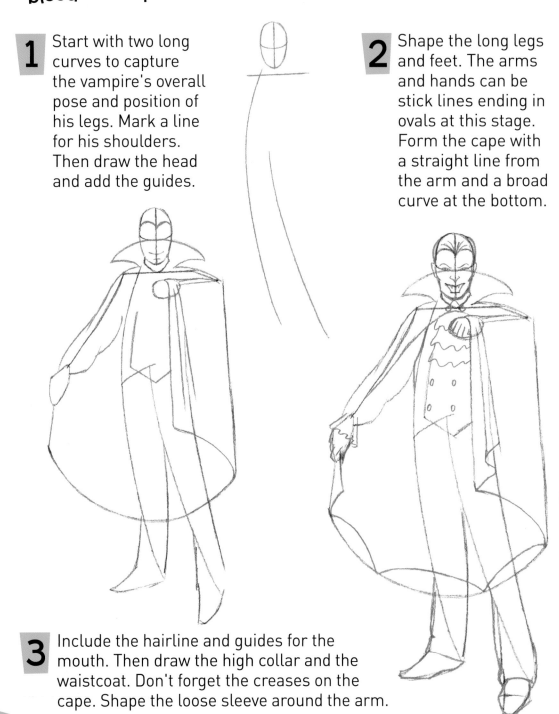

3 Include the hairline and guides for the mouth. Then draw the high collar and the waistcoat. Don't forget the creases on the cape. Shape the loose sleeve around the arm.

4 Finally, fill in the face and hair, and shape the sunken cheeks. Include the shirt frills and waistcoat buttons. When you have given the cape a curvy edge, rub out the guide.

5 Much of the colour here is solid black. The cape has two shades of red. By adding pale blue highlights, you can create the effect of a ghostly moonlit glow!

TOP TIPS

To capture a vampire's hynoptic character, you need to spend time on the face details.

Draw cat-like eyes and heavy eyebrows. Colour the eyes fiery orange and yellow, then paint dark red around the rims for a spooky look.

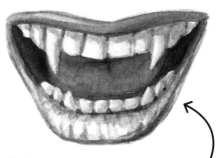

Make the lips pale so that the teeth stand out. The fangs should be pointed and slightly curved. Use yellow for the shading.

Mad scientist

Yikes! What is this crazy cartoon scientist inventing this time? What's bubbling in his lab? Once you've mastered him mixing his chemicals, try drawing the explosion that comes next!

1 Draw two overlapping circles, one large and one small, for the big head. Then add a guideline down the centre. A cone shape forms the body.

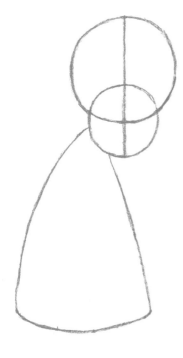

2 Next copy the arms and legs. They are made up of simple lines and shapes so should be easy to draw. Outline the massive hair and the pointed hairline.

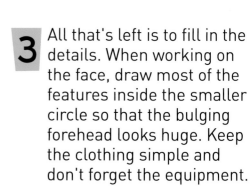

3 All that's left is to fill in the details. When working on the face, draw most of the features inside the smaller circle so that the bulging forehead looks huge. Keep the clothing simple and don't forget the equipment.

4
When colouring in, use drab browns and greys for the scientist's hair and most of his clothing. Contrast this with whacky yellow gloves and toxic pink and lime green chemicals.

CARTOON CORNER

A crazy scientist needs some crazy equipment! Why not bring his lab to life as well?

A red face with puffed-out cheeks and scrunched up eyes makes this flask look like it's about to explode at any moment.

This test tube is on the loose. Give it waving stick arms, running legs and a cheeky face. A few drops spilling out of the top help, too.

Horrible orc

Orcs are fierce humanoid monsters with grotesque features. In this drawing, your goal is to capture the beast's bulky shape and his mean, but dim, expression.

1 Start with a large circle for the shoulders and overall body shape. Another circle inside forms the stomach and three smaller circles mark the hands and the head.

2 On the bottom edge of the largest circle, draw two more circles for the knees and add lines for the powerful legs and large feet. Start to draw the arms.

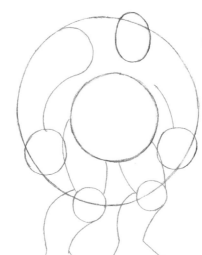

3 Work on the arms to give them a muscly look and draw the chest armour. Mark the guidelines for the face and the sword.

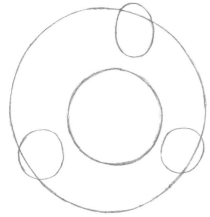

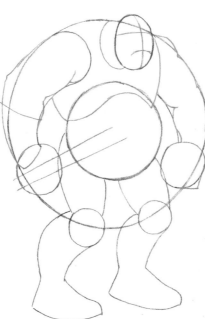

4 Bring your orc to life by completing his accessories including his cuff, kneepads and boots. Shape his hands and finish off his face. Rub out the circular guide.

5 You want an orc to look grimy, so colour him in yucky greens and yellows with a hint of purple. Make his armour look dull with different shades of brown.

TOP TIPS

Follow these tips to add the finishing touches to your beast.

Copy the shape of the sword carefully, then add a Celtic design to the handle and blade. Look in books for other Celtic designs you could use.

Make the head a dome shape and the eyes narrow. Paint your skin colours on top of each other in splodges to create a mottled effect.

Sea witch

In folklore, sea witches had power over the waves. When drawing this wicked-looking creature, remember that she is half human and half serpent.

1 Draw three basic shapes – a small circle for the head, an oval for the chest and a large circle for the serpent body. Then add guidelines for the shoulders and arms.

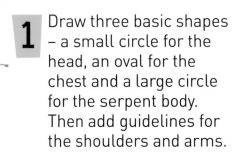

2 When shaping the arms and shoulders, spend time on the muscles. Work on the body and tail following the curve of the circle. Outline the face and add the trident.

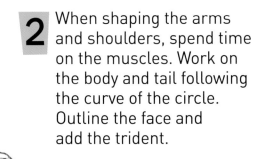

3 Shape the body and tail further. Give the sea witch a seashell helmet and top, and flowing hair. Then add her face. Finish off the hands and the trident. Rub out the circular guide.

4 Before colouring in, add fins to the arms and webbing to the fingers to make the creature truly fishy. Sea greens and blues work well for the body, along with a golden shell hat.

CARTOON CORNER

Draw and colour a seahorse chariot for your wicked witch in three simple steps.

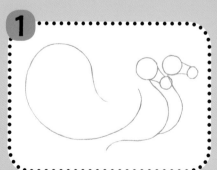

1 Form the seahorses using curved lines for the bodies and circles for the heads. Work on the one nearest to you first. Then shape the chariot.

2 Add the reins to the seahorses and slot in their face details. Finish off their curly tails. Scallop the edge of the chariot and draw the cushion.

3 You can add more detail at the inking stage, such as ridges on the seahorses' bodies. Make the inside of the chariot golden yellow.

FANTASY CHARACTERS
Elf princess

Make this elfin princess with pointed ears look tall and elegant rather than strong and muscular. Use lots of flowing, curved lines to achieve this graceful effect.

1 Start with a long, curved line running through the whole body to get the right pose. Then draw ovals for the head, chest and hips. Mark the shoulders and face guides.

2 Add dots for the knees, and a guideline for the front leg. The feet can be simple shapes for now. Position the arms and hands, paying attention to the angles.

3 Shape the body, starting with the chest and arm. A bell shape forms the skirt. Below, draw the legs and boots. Add pointed ears and flowing hair. Mark the facial features.

4 When finishing off, pay attention to the face and hands. Make the fingers long and thin. Complete the costume including the pleated skirt, and work on the face and hair. Add a flower as a final touch.

5 Colour your princess in shades of green for a woodland feel. Keep the shading light and gentle. Accessorize her with gold or silver jewellery.

TOP TIPS

Try drawing your princess in profile instead. Here are some tips on creating delicate elfin features.

Give her a long face and a slender, upturned nose. Make her lips small but full and her eyebrows thin and arched. Her cheeks should have a rosy glow.

Viking warrior

This fantasy Viking warrior is fierce and strong. You can capture this by giving him a broad body and setting his muscular legs wide apart in a fighting stance.

1 First draw a large X shape. Using this as your guide, position a box for the body and a circle for the head. Then add guidelines for one arm ending in an oval for the hand.

2 Next outline the body, making sure that the arms and legs look muscular. Mark the knee joints and the face guides. Start the shield.

3 Now start adding the details. Copy the picture or invent your own face, costume and weapons. Just remember to make your warrior look dangerous!

4 Think about the different textures when inking and colouring in. Give the fur boots fluffy edges, make the wooden shield hard and the metal clasps shiny.

CARTOON CORNER

Different warriors need different helmets. Check out these designs.

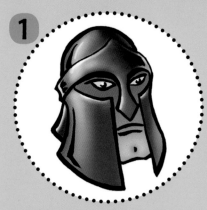

1 A full face protector makes this Spartan warrior look really scary. It also makes his eyes stand out.

2 This knight's helmet is more decorative. Make the metal shine with white highlights and add brass clips.

3 How about drawing a Roman centurion? Check out history books for more picture references.

The next step

SCIENCE LAB

The mad scientist you drew (pages 82-3) needs his own lab to experiment in! Have a go at copying this picture using the hints and tips to bring the cartoon scene to life.

Make the objects in the lab smaller the farther away they are.

Add a ceiling in a different colour so it looks like the scientist is inside a room.

Don't forget to include shadows under the shelves to make them seem real and solid.

Leaving lots of space around a character helps it to stand out.

Set tools and objects at angles to make the picture more interesting.

Get creative in a cartoon picture. Who's to say that a test tube or a bunsen burner shouldn't have a face?!

SPEED MACHINES

You'll discover all kinds of thrilling vehicles to draw in this chapter and learn techniques to improve your technical drawing skills. So sharpen your pencils and get your ruler out now!

Sports car
Work with a grid to build up this shiny, sleek sports car. Then customize it any way you want.

Jet plane
Triangles and lines form the basis of this supersonic jet with a blazing smoke trail.

Motorbike
Design a streamlined superbike with chunky wheels, then add a rider.

Speedboat
Draw a sleek speedboat, then show it speeding through the water.

Biplane
As well as this curved biplane, discover how to draw a cartoon jumbo jet.

Sports car

For this turbo-charged sports car, you're going to start with a simple box grid. This will help you to position the curves and get the angle of the drawing just right.

1 Use a ruler to measure the lengths of the lines and the distances they are apart. The top line should be straight and the lines below increasingly angled.

2 Now draw the curved shape of the car, beginning with the roof and bonnet. Follow the grid carefully. Draw three vertical lines to position the wheels.

3 Work on the front and bottom, adding the grille shape and wheel arches. Draw a straight line to mark the ground. Shape the windscreen and side window.

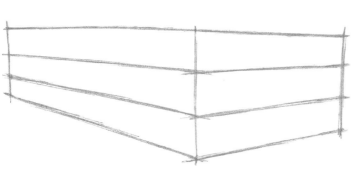

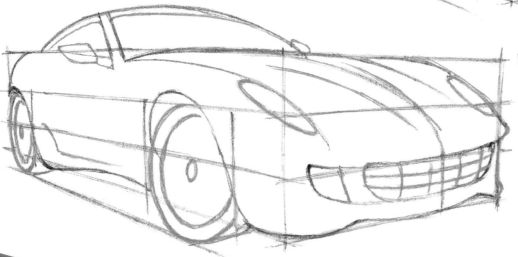

4 Take time over the wheels, noticing how the front one is rounder than the back one. Position them between the same grid lines. Then add the wing mirrors, grille and headlights. Rub out the grid.

5 Bold red is the perfect colour for a sports car. Keep the shading smooth and add white highlights for a sleek, shiny finish. Shade in the road too.

TOP TIPS

Customize your car with a few simple tweaks. As well as the hubcaps and headlights shown here, think about adding go-faster stripes, badges and a personalized number plate.

Give your car class with these star-shaped alloy hubcaps. Blend grey into white to make them look shiny. For chunky tyres, make the edges jagged.

Headlights can be round, oval or tube-shaped like these. Colour the bulb pale yellow and add hazy beams of light with blurred edges.

Formula 1 car

This mean speed machine is made up of lots of different shapes. Draw each one in the right position and your cartoon racing car will soon be zooming along!

1 Start with three horizontal straight lines. Then draw three egg shapes for the wheels. Make them tilt slightly inwards. Add the top of the fourth wheel, following the guidelines.

2 Draw a long curve for the bonnet and shape the aerofoil at the front. Add a domed helmet and the back of the seat. Take care to work accurately. Next draw two more guides for the rear aerofoil.

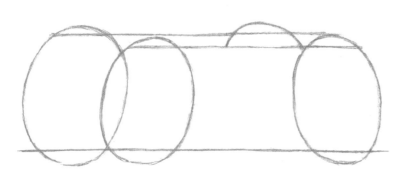

3 Concentrate hard and copy all the shapes here to finish off your drawing. Pay attention to how they fit into the guides. Keep your lines straight and wheel curves sloping for a cartoon feel. Then rub out the guides.

4 To make the body of the car bright and shiny, use white highlights around the edges. Make the tyres look duller with grey highlights.

CARTOON CORNER

Try drawing another cartoon car, then give it a face to make it really come alive!

1

2

3

Sketch this simple small car. Follow the positioning of the lights, seats and grille as these will become the facial features.

Now change the headlights and grille into eyes and a mouth! Shade in the pupils and draw teeth. Keep the seats plain.

For this cartoon car face, change the wing mirrors into ears and make windscreen wiper eyes! Don't forget the gnashing teeth.

Jet plane

Get ready to launch a supersonic jet into the air! This drawing has lots of straight lines, so use a ruler and measure accurately. It will really help to get a great end result.

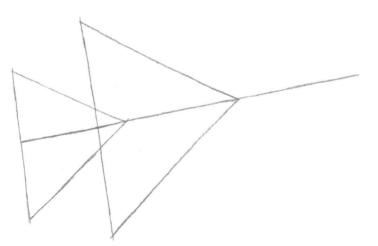

1 Start with a long, straight centre line at a slight angle. Then draw two different-sized triangles. Make sure they both sit on the centre line so they are symmetrical.

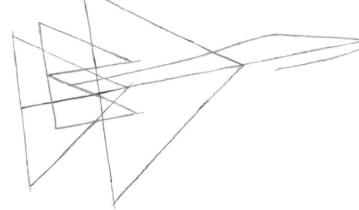

2 Working with the centre line again, draw two right-angled triangles for the twin tail fins. Next, outline the fuselage, or body, making sure you curl the nose.

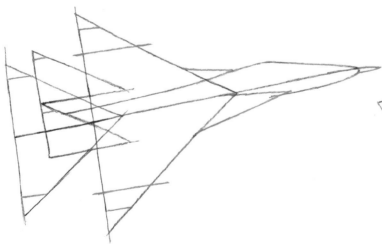

3 Draw parallel lines over the wings, tail and fins to help you trim the edges and position the engines. Complete the wing shape and add the pointed nose cone.

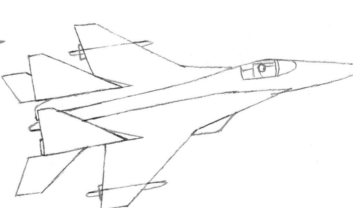

4 Rub out the tops of the fins and the edges of the wings and tail, following the guides. The drawing should be much simpler now, so it will be easy to add the final touches.

5 Use a striking colour scheme for your jet. Don't forget to add smoke trails for a sense of speed and drama.

TOP TIPS

Check out how to draw a realistic smoke trail. This will make your aerobatic plane look like it's speeding across the sky and add a real sense of drama to your picture.

Turn a soft pencil on its side and make lots of circular movements with the lead to form a cloud shape. Leave the centre white.

For a more whispy effect, use a small piece of charcoal. Smudge the trail edges with your fingertips to make them look soft.

Stunt biplane

Old-fashioned biplanes are fantastic at twisting and turning in the sky. Get out your pens and draw this cartoon version complete with whacky pilot!

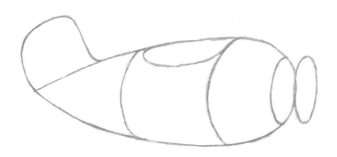

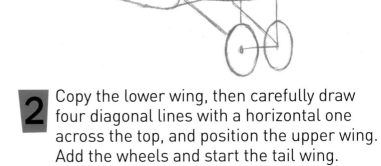

1 Draw a torpedo shape for the plane's body. Add a narrow oval for the propellor and shape the tail. Form the cockpit with several curved lines.

2 Copy the lower wing, then carefully draw four diagonal lines with a horizontal one across the top, and position the upper wing. Add the wheels and start the tail wing.

3 Now finish off the wing and wheel struts, and complete the tail wing. Work on the propellor and fill out the wheels. Finally draw your pilot with his old-fashioned headgear, goggles and flowing scarf.

4 Why not choose a different colour scheme for your plane? Or how about giving the body a camouflage design?

CARTOON CORNER

Instead of a tiny biplane, try drawing a massive jumbo jet instead!

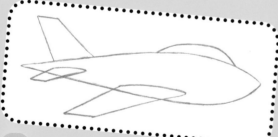

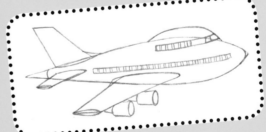

2 Soften the outline and thicken the wing edges. Add the windows and the two engines beneath the wings.

1 This time start with a much longer torpedo shape. Add a curve on top to make the plane take on the shape of a jumbo jet. Draw the wings and tail.

3 Finally, work on the colouring. Jumbo jets are usually white with blocks of colour here and there. Include a design for the tail.

Speedboat

Your challenge with this futuristic speedboat is to make it look streamlined. Take care with the overall shape and add curved designs in a contrasting colour to achieve the effect.

1 First draw this simple grid. It will help you to get the perspective and angle of your boat just right. Notice how the short lines across are slightly curved.

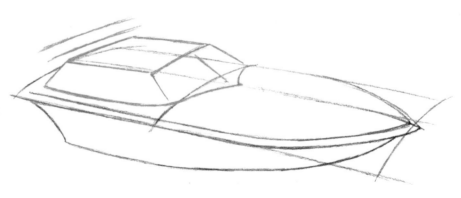

2 Draw a short curve following the centre line of the grid to mark the front point of the boat. Then shape the deck using the the rest of the grid. Draw the hull below.

3 Now outline the cabin area including the windows. Angle the lines dividing the windows inwards, towards the roof. Add two lines at the back of the cabin to position the aerofoil.

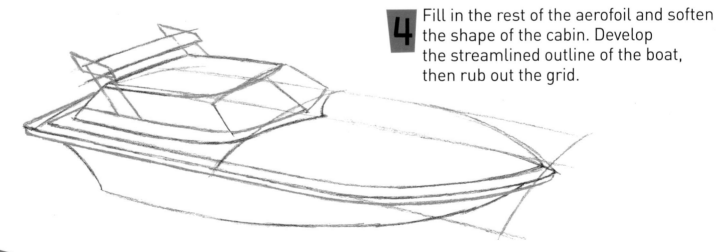

4 Fill in the rest of the aerofoil and soften the shape of the cabin. Develop the streamlined outline of the boat, then rub out the grid.

5 When inking the outline, make the shape of the windows more curved. Use a slightly different colour shade from the main body of the boat.

TOP TIPS

Why not draw your speedboat powering through the water!
Add splashing waves and a foamy spray to complete the picture.

Try using watercolour paints in shades of blue for your waves. To create the white spray effect, dab your paintbrush rather than using long strokes.

Superbike

When drawing this cartoon superbike, concentrate hard on getting the shapes and lines right in the first step. After that, everything should fall into place!

1 Copy the two chunky wheels. Make the one on the right larger so it seems nearer. Draw the straight lines leading off the front wheel and add the three curved lines.

2 With the guides in place, develop the bodywork including the seat and exhaust pipe. Follow the picture carefully and watch how the bike starts to take shape.

3 All that's left now is to work on the details. Position the wheel discs and guards carefully. Then draw the handlebar and headlights. Finish off the exhaust pipe.

4 Before colouring in, go over your outline with a black felt-tip pen using long unbroken strokes. This will help make the bike look really sleek.

CARTOON CORNER

Every motorbike needs a super-slick rider! Here's how to draw one for your incredible speed machine.

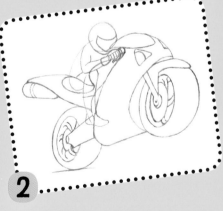

1 Start with a circle for the helmet. Then draw the curve of the rider's back, shape his leg and position his hand.

2 Finish off the rider's helmet and his body. For an extra touch, raise the bike's front wheel off the ground and change the angle at the bottom.

3 Use one block colour for a streamlined rider and add sparkly highlights to the bike's body to make it gleam.

Bullet train

Draw this bullet train in perspective so that it gets smaller the further away it is and disappears into the distance. This will give your picture a real sense of drama and speed.

Horizon

1 Start with a series of lines that join together at the vanishing point on the horizon line. Curve them slightly to show the bend in the track.

2 Next add vertical lines, making sure that they are straight. Space them so that they get closer together towards the end. The first line marks the front of the train.

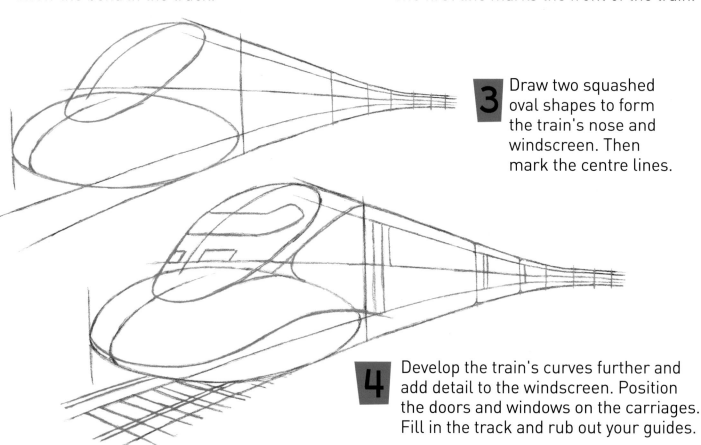

3 Draw two squashed oval shapes to form the train's nose and windscreen. Then mark the centre lines.

4 Develop the train's curves further and add detail to the windscreen. Position the doors and windows on the carriages. Fill in the track and rub out your guides.

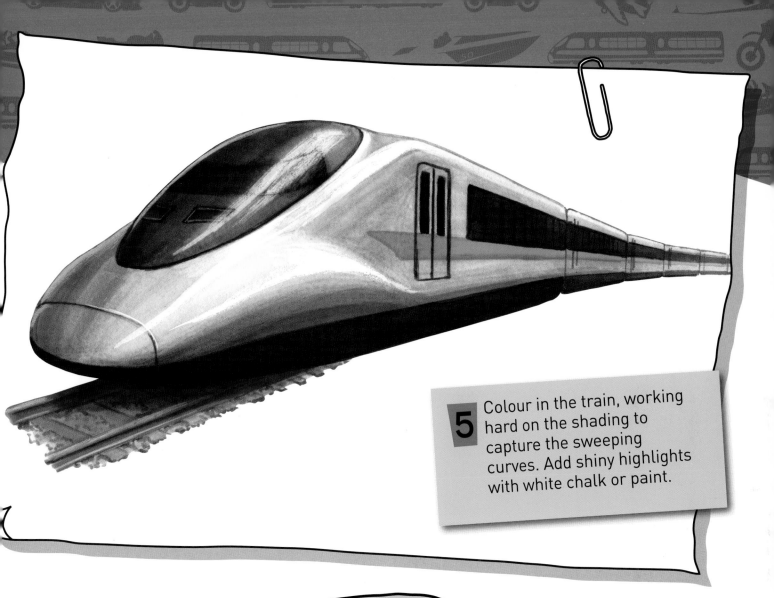

5 Colour in the train, working hard on the shading to capture the sweeping curves. Add shiny highlights with white chalk or paint.

TOP TIPS

Make your railway track look as realistic as your train! Colour the metal rails rusty orange and the wooden sleepers pinkish-grey. Don't forget to include the metal rivets.

For the pebbly ground, you could use a sand-coloured wash with black and grey stones on top.

Space shuttle

This space shuttle has huge rockets and a giant fuel tank to blast it into space. Follow the steps to launch your cartoon version into the air!

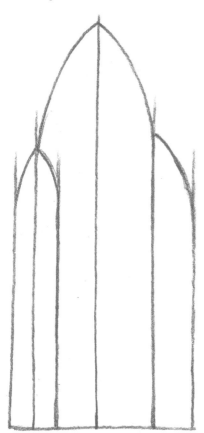

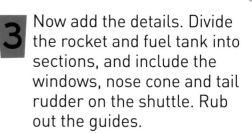

1 Draw the centre line first so that you can make the curves on the large arch shape symmetrical. Then add the outer shapes.

2 The large arch is the fuel tank and the thin arch, a rocket. Outline the shape of the space shuttle on the right. Draw curves for the bottom of the shuttle and the rocket.

3 Now add the details. Divide the rocket and fuel tank into sections, and include the windows, nose cone and tail rudder on the shuttle. Rub out the guides.

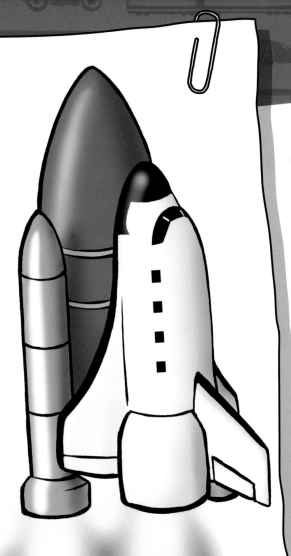

4 Take care over the shading to make the space shuttle seem like a solid object. Even though the main colour is white, introduce blue-grey to darken the edges.

CARTOON CORNER

Try drawing two different types of spaceship. Then use one of the characters from page 61 to create a comic strip!

1

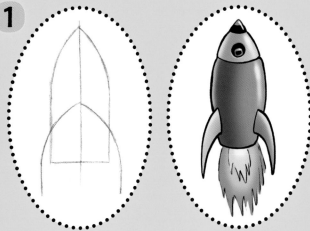

This cone-shaped spaceship is based on two arch shapes. You can choose any colour scheme but be sure to include bright orange and yellow flames to power the spaceship along.

2

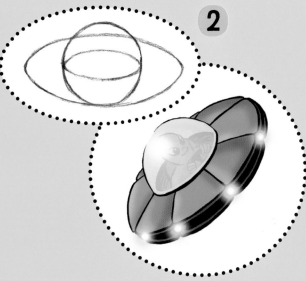

To draw a flying saucer, start with a ball and add an oval inside. The top half of the ball is the dome of the ship. Then draw another oval for the outer edge. Experiment with different angles.

The next step

ON THE RACETRACK

Try using the sports car you drew (pages 94-5) to design a thrilling race scene. You can also use some of the techniques here for showing other speed machines on the move.

A deep blue sky provides contrast to the dark and intense racetrack.

Make the cars bright and shiny so they stand out on the page.

Blur the crowd so the focus is firmly on the race itself.

Use long, sweeping strokes on the track and add skid marks to create a sense of movement.

Dark shadows underneath both cars tie them together and make the race seem very close.

You can base your cars on the same design but change their features and the colour of the paintwork.

DINOSAURS

In this section, discover how to draw dinosaurs! From gentle plant-eaters to ferocious meat-eaters and armoured beasts, there's sure to be a dinosaur to suit you.

T. rex
Follow the steps to create your very own T. rex with terrifying teeth and claws.

Velociraptor
Get out your pens and tackle vicious Velociraptor.

Brachiosaurs
Try drawing long-necked Brachiosaurus munching on some leaves.

Triceratops
Freak out your friends when you draw Triceratops with its horns and neck plate.

Archaeopteryx
Is it a bird? Is it a dinosaur? No, it's Archaeopteryx! Learn how to draw this Jurassic bird.

Tyrannosaurus rex

Follow the steps to draw the most terrifying dinosaur of them all - bone-crunching T. rex. Work hard at getting the shape of the body right with all its knobbly bumps and curves.

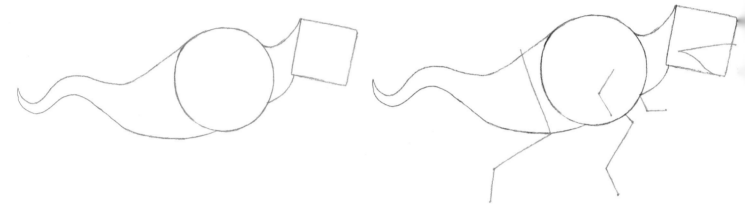

1 Draw a big circle for the body and work outwards to shape the neck and tail. Notice how the thick tail tapers to a point. A box shape forms T. rex's head.

2 The legs and arms are quite tricky so start with stick drawings. Copy the picture carefully, paying attention to the line lengths and angles. Then shape the mouth.

3 Now work on the shape of the legs. Make them chunky at the thighs and include bulging muscles. The arms should be short and skinny. Develop the mouth further.

4 Finally add the details. Work on the face including the two bumps at the top of the head and add a guideline for the teeth. Shape the feet, hands and bumpy back.

5 Use a thick pen to outline the bulky body and colour in the beast. Heavy shading, especially under the eyes and around the jaw, adds a menacing effect.

TOP TIPS

Check out these tips on how to finish off the sharp bits — the teeth and claws!

Your T. rex needs lots and lots of teeth to munch its dinner. Work with a fine pen to draw them accurately and to provide a contrast to the heavier body outline.

When drawing the claws, make them long and curved to show how they can grab prey. Blend orange into cream to make them look really grubby!

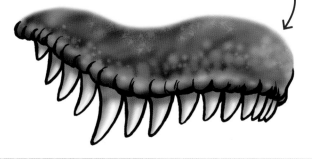

Velociraptor

Velociraptor may not have been very large dinosaur, but it sure was vicious! Have a go at drawing this cartoon creation including those lethal toe claws.

1 Start off with a crescent shape for the body and tail, swooping round to make the curves. Draw three swift strokes to form the pointed head.

2 Add the legs and arms, paying attention to the position of the curving lines. Add a triangle on top of the head for the crest feathers, and develop the end of the tail.

3 Velociraptors were cunning creatures so try to capture this as you finish off the face. Then shape the feet and sharp claws. When working on the outline, add feathery edges to the arms, head crest and tail.

4 When colouring in, go for a dramatic effect. This picture has bold orange and brown stripes based on a tiger's coat, but you could try a different animal pattern.

CARTOON CORNER

Adapt your character to create a hatching baby Velociraptor.

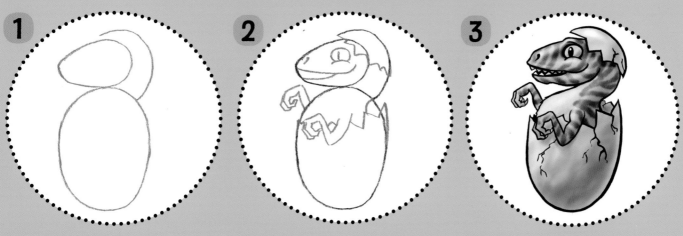

1 Draw an upright oval for the egg and a more pointed one on its side for the dino's head. Join them with a curve.

2 Work on the the cute face and shape the grasping arms. Add jagged lines to show where the egg has cracked.

3 Give the baby dino its teeth and colour it in as before. Choose a shade for the egg and add fine crack lines.

Iguanodon

Iguanodon was a large plant-eater with two unusual thumb spikes. Here, you are working in a realistic style. Give the dinosaur a mottled skin to show that it is a reptile.

1 Begin with a tilted egg shape for the body. Then shape the thick swishing tail. Remember to curl it at the end. A long curved line starts to form the neck.

2 Next shape the arms and the legs, remembering that this dinosaur stands almost upright. Draw a box for the head and another curved line for the back of the neck.

3 Outline the hands and feet, then shape the face and neck flap. When you add the thumb spikes and beak-like mouth, Iguanodon will really come to life.

4 Finally work on the details. Include bulges for the knee joints and draw curving fingers. Shape the body a little more to show its strength and finish off the mouth.

5 Colour the creature in pale shades with felt-tip pens. Then shade over the top with a pencil and smudge the edges. This will help make your dinosaur look really realistic.

TOP TIPS

Pay attention to the details to give your image more impact.

Below the eye, draw spiralling lines. This will make the skin seem leathery.

Make Iguanodon's fingers slender and knobbly. Contrast this with the wide, smooth thumb spike.

Brachiosaurus

This cartoon Brachiosaurus is really easy to draw. What's more, no one really knows what colour dinosaurs were so choose any colour scheme you want to finish it off!

1 First draw a long banana shape. Around this, add two bulging curves. These form the dinosaur's body, tail and long neck.

2 Next plot out the wide thighs with two U-shaped curves. Finish off the tail and shape the tiny head at the top of the neck.

3 Now add the lower legs. Flatten out the ends to make jokey oversized feet and draw the toes. In contrast, the head should be tiny with lots of personality. When rubbing out the guidelines, be sure to leave the domed head crest.

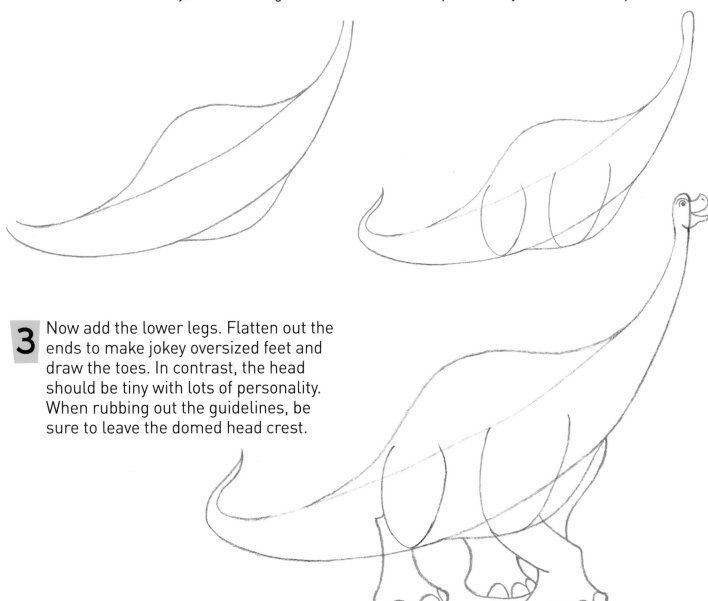

4 When colouring your cartoon dinosaur, go whacky and wild! Instead of spots, try a rainbow effect or bright neon spirals.

CARTOON CORNER

How about giving your dinosaur a snack to chew on or a footprint trail?

1

Brachiosaurus munched on leaves and twigs from the tree-tops, reaching them with its long neck. When you draw its snack, make it look like a plant from Jurassic times!

Brachiosaurus had wide feet. Try using a photo of an elephant's footprint for reference to show a dusty trail on the ground.

2

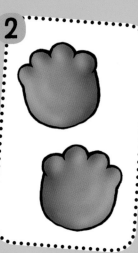

Triceratops

With its pointed horns and giant neck plate, Triceratops looked fierce, but this gentle giant only munched plants. Follow the steps to draw its bulky, leathery frame.

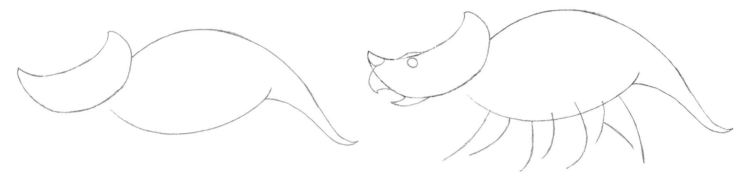

1 Draw a crescent moon shape for the head and neck plate. Then copy the rest of the picture to form the body and tail. Make the the head quite big in relation to the body.

2 Develop the head further by outlining the nose horn and the beak-shaped mouth. Don't forget to add the eye. A series of curved lines start the chunky legs.

3 Now shape the tops of the legs with more curved lines making sure they look thick and muscly, and add the wide feet. Draw two long pointed horns above the eye.

4 Work on the Triceratops' neckline and bottom of the mouth. Add a nostril and wrinkle lines to give the dinosaur its character. Finish off by drawing the toes.

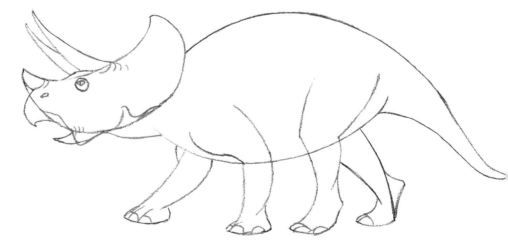

5 When colouring in, use lots of curved lines to bring out the wrinkly elephant-like skin. Work in shades of brown and white. For shading tips, go to pages 12–13.

TOP TIPS

Make your picture look even more professional with these artists' tips.

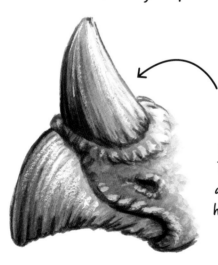

To make the horn on Triceratops' nose stand out from the rest of the body, work mainly in a yellowish-brown colour. Then add dark shading at the bottom and white highlights at the top.

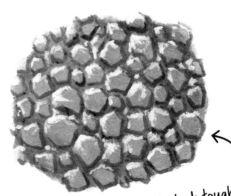

You can make Triceratops' skin look tough and scaly by drawing lots of small uneven shapes. Colour the gaps a darker brown than the shapes.

Ankylosaurus

Pick up your pencils and try drawing this Ankylosaurus with its swinging club tail. Ankylosaurus used its bony tail to defend itself from larger meat-eating dinosaurs.

1 Start with a giant teardrop shape for the body and tail. Then draw a swooping curve to mark the edge of the back and neck armour. A triangle forms the head armour.

2 Next shape the head and neck, and add the face details. Give Ankylosaurus a friendly expression. Work on the legs and feet, and draw two circles for the club at the end of the tail.

3 A grid across the back will help you to position the bony armour. Draw pebble shapes on top of it, then rub out the grid. Finally, add a cheek spike to the face and finish off the toes.

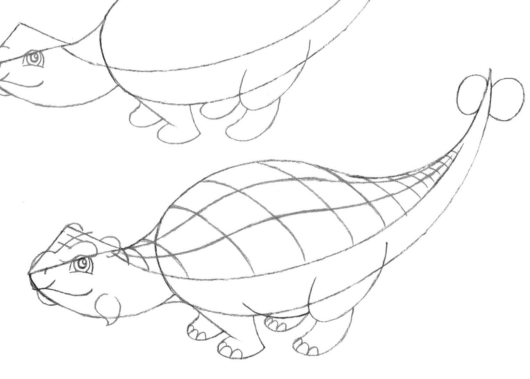

4 Giving the dinosaur a thick, dark outline will help to make it look powerful. It's also a good idea to use contrasting colours for the armour and the body.

CARTOON CORNER

Want to show your Ankylosaurus in full swing? Then follow the steps below!

1

2

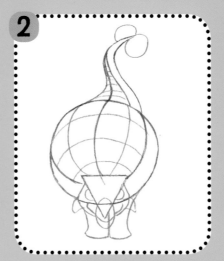

3

The dinosaur is facing you, so draw a circle for the body and a triangle pointing downwards for the head armour. Copy the rest of the picture.

As before, add the grid for the body armour and the two circles for the tail. Then work on the face shape and the two wide, front legs.

Colour your dinosaur like the main picture or choose something different. Add swishing lines to show the movement of the tail and body.

Archaeopteryx

Archaeopteryx was a small prehistoric flying creature that lived at the time of the dinosaurs. Work hard to capture its feathered bird-like wings and scaly dinosaur-like feet and claws.

1 Draw a rugby ball shape for Archaeopteryx's body. Add a small oval for the head and join the two shapes together to form the neck.

2 Next work on the wing shape. Copy the picture carefully so the top of the wings look symmetrical. Then draw in the legs and tail, and add the eye and beak.

3 Outline the bottom of the wings and the feathered tail. Make the tail look like a paddle for now. Mark the position of the feet and wing claws.

4 The final step is to work on the details. Create the feathers with smooth, curved lines. Shape the scaly feet and add the claws. Add detail to the eye too.

5 Rub out the guidelines, then go over the feathers and the body with a fine black pen. Use lots of short delicate lines around the neck and leg area to suggest a fluffier texture here.

TOP TIPS

Feathers and scaly feet give Archaeopteryx its unique character. Here's how to draw and colour them in close-up.

For the wings, lay down a watercolour base in green and blue first. Then on top, shade with coloured pencils. This will create a feathery effect.

When drawing the feet, add oval shapes with a fine black pen to create scales. Colour the feet yellowish brown.

Dimetrodon

With its huge sail fin, sharp teeth and crocodile-like body, Dimetrodon was a fearsome land predator that lived about 280 million years ago. Get ready to draw this beast!

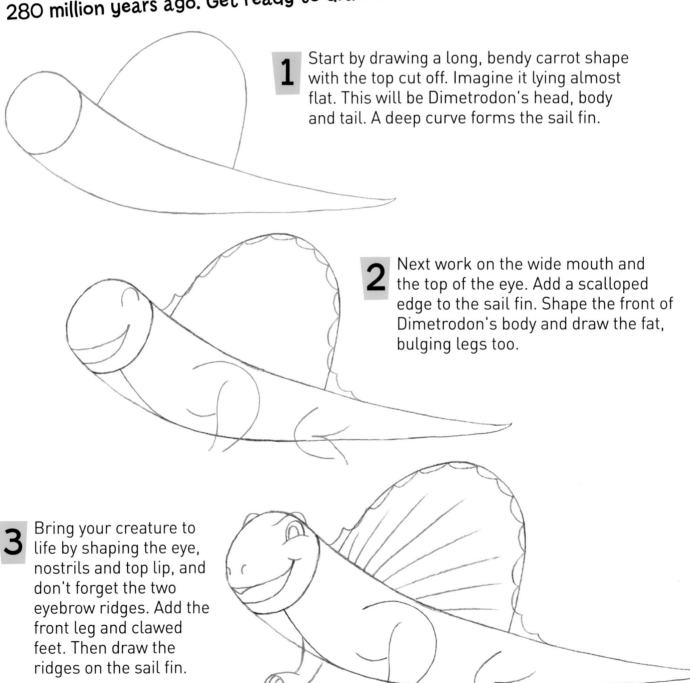

1 Start by drawing a long, bendy carrot shape with the top cut off. Imagine it lying almost flat. This will be Dimetrodon's head, body and tail. A deep curve forms the sail fin.

2 Next work on the wide mouth and the top of the eye. Add a scalloped edge to the sail fin. Shape the front of Dimetrodon's body and draw the fat, bulging legs too.

3 Bring your creature to life by shaping the eye, nostrils and top lip, and don't forget the two eyebrow ridges. Add the front leg and clawed feet. Then draw the ridges on the sail fin.

4 Once you've drawn the teeth, you can choose any colour scheme or pattern for Dimetrodon. Try blending in an extra colour on the sail fin to make it stand out.

CARTOON CORNER

There's more than one way to draw Dimetrodon!

1

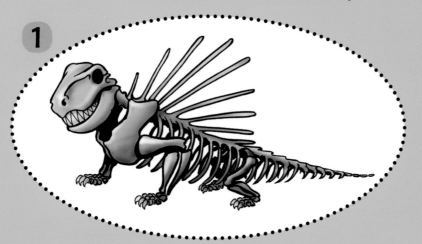

2

Draw its skeleton and you'll look like a real dinosaur expert. Make the ribcage long and add ridges to the tail. The skull should be large and solid while the bones in the sail fin need to be slender. Go over the outline with a fine black pen, then colour the picture greyish-brown.

Draw a baby Dimetrodon. Work with an S-shape and include a short tail and sail fin. Add a prop, like a bone, to give the dinosaur personality.

The next step

PREHISTORIC PARK

Place your dinosaurs in a dramatic scene. We've used T. rex (pages 112-13), Velociraptor (pages 114-15), Brachiosaurus (pages 118-19) and Ankylosaurus (pages 122-23) but you could choose different ones.

Notice how all the dinosaurs' eyes are looking towards T. rex to give the scene a focus.

Make the forest darker in the middle to create a sense of distance.

Frame your picture with plants, trees and leaves.

Vary the shapes of the leaves to make the picture more interesting.

Items in the foreground appear larger than those further back.

Hide the dinosaurs' feet and legs among the leaves to create different layers in the picture.